Moving Forward in Hope

A DEVOTIONAL FOR FAMILIES OF LGBTQ+ LOVED ONES

DENISE SHICK

LIVING STONES
MINISTRIES

HELP4FAMILIES
MINISTRY

Moving Forward in Hope: A Devotional for Families of LGBTQ+ Loved Ones

Contents

Dear Loving God,

I ask You to meet each person right where they are in their journey. May they hear Your small still voice as You speak, minister, and strengthen them. I pray that any doubt they may have about who You are, the power You possess, or the promises You've given be countered by Your gracious comfort and love.

Enable each person to build a strong house of faith to withstand the Enemy's lies. Remove the confusion and chaos he creates to hurt them and drive them away from You and the faith they proclaim and live by.

May the words from Proverbs 3:5—"Trust in the Lord with all your heart"— be firmly planted in their soul and mind.

Minister to each one. May they draw closer to You and stronger in faith as they travel through their personal journey.

In Jesus' name I pray, amen.

Reflect Jesus

Clothe yourself with compassion, kindness, humility, gentleness, and patience.

—Colossians 3:12

After Julie arrived home from a difficult day at work, she began to prepare dinner. Soon her husband, Aaron, entered the kitchen. As they shared about their workdays, their son Michael walked into the house.

"Did basketball practice run late?" Aaron asked.

Michael nodded, then muttered something unintelligible.

"I didn't hear you, son," Julie said.

"I have something to tell you," he said. "You better sit down."

Julie's throat tightened, and her heart felt heavy as she pulled a chair away from the kitchen table and sat. Aaron slid into the seat next to her and reached for her hand.

Michael glanced at them both, then looked toward the window. His voice trembled as he said, "I'm gay. I know being gay is not something you support, and that's why it's been so hard to tell you."

An earthquake seemed to rumble under Julie's feet. A weight in her chest made it hard to breathe, much less speak.

Aaron's voice was husky with emotion as he said, "Michael, we love you. We want to know more about why you think you're gay. We realize how difficult it was to tell us, and we can only imagine how you're feeling. But more than anything, we want you to know that we love you." He took a deep breath. "As hard as this is to say, Mom and I don't believe this is God's best for you. We hope you'll allow us to hear your feelings and thoughts and to walk with you as you seek answers. Others may tell you that we don't love you. But we do, and we always will, no matter what."

The heart-wrenching announcement of a loved one identifying gay or transgender is spoken in the homes of Christian families at an alarming rate. Of course our immediate response is usually shock and disbelief. But the words we speak at such a time are crucial, and venting our anger or dismay may drive our loved one away.

In Colossians 3, Paul outlines how we should respond to others no matter how deeply their words or choices hurt us. God intricately knit every human being in the womb (Psalm 139:13). He asks us to treat every single person the way He intended—as His beloved, beautiful, unique creation. Reflect Jesus' compassion as you interact with your loved one. No matter how devastated you may feel right now, demonstrate kindness, humility, gentleness, and patience.

Today's Choice: Read Colossians 3:12–17. What action can you take today that will demonstrate God's love in a tangible way? Two possibilities: prepare a favorite food or send a thinking-of-you card or text.

Reflections:

_____

_____

_____

_____

_____

Crumbling Walls

"My thoughts are nothing like your thoughts," says the Lord. "And my ways are far beyond anything you could imagine. For just as the heavens are higher than the earth, so my ways are higher than your ways and my thoughts higher than your thoughts."

—Isaiah 55: 8–9 (NLT)

How can you continue to trust God when the walls of your life crumble, leaving you exposed and defenseless?

Jesus said, "In this world you will have trouble" (John 16:33). I wrestled with this truth when I examined the rubble of plans and dreams that surrounded me when my father left to become Becky and for many years afterward as he clung to his fantasy world.

Sometimes the rumble of pain moves through us like an earthquake, violently shaking the truth that we built our life on. Maybe you felt that way when your loved one announced their LGBTQ+ identity, then asked you to celebrate it by accepting their same-sex partner or their gender transition. Maybe your spouse asked for a divorce or, worse, wanted you to embrace his or her new identity and remain married.

God doesn't always do what we expect Him to do. Following Him on an unknown journey is frightening, especially after the ground beneath you has crumbled, and the God who permitted the earthquake now whispers, "Let Me hold you, let Me lead you."

It's difficult to balance the truth of God's unchanging, unconditional love with His willingness to allow pain to upend our lives—especially the kind of pain that knocks you to the ground and leaves you gasping for breath.

Beneath all the fear and questions in my soul about my dad, though, I heard Jesus' quiet, calm voice: "Trust Me with all your heart. Look up toward heaven even though the ground under your feet is trembling." At that point, I had to choose. Would I stay stuck in my pain, questions, and disappointment, or would I move forward with God by trusting Him in spite of unanswered questions and unhealed wounds?

Too often, trying to find some assurance in life's uncertainty, we attempt to force-fit the God of the universe into a box small enough for our finite minds to comprehend. But doing this strips away the mystery and wonder that make Him God, that make Him worthy of our trust and worship. I don't understand how my car works—or my computer or my phone—but I still use them every day. I turn to them again and again when I need them, and I don't ever demand an explanation for how they operate. So why do I think I need to understand everything God does?

Walls crumble. Dreams evaporate. God says, "Trust me anyway." Will you continue to question Him, or will you allow Him to lead you out of the rubble?

> **Today's Choice:** Read Isaiah 55. What invitation does God give in verses 1–3? What promises are given in verses 6–7 and 10–13? How can applying those promises to your situation help you trust God in spite of your pain?

Reflections:

_____

_____

_____

_____

_____

So Many Tears

You keep track of all my sorrows. You have collected all my tears in your bottle. You have recorded each one in your book.

—Psalm 56:8 (NLT)

The day grew warm in the afternoon sun, so Serena asked Mom if she and her younger brothers could play outside. Mom said, "Grab your sweaters" as Serena, Ricky, and Paul darted from the living room to the patio door.

First they kicked around a soccer ball, then they switched to freeze tag. Serena agreed to be It first. She chased her brothers round and round the backyard. When she finally touched Paul's shoulder, all three fell to the ground laughing.

Dad called out from the garage: "Serena, go get the hot dogs, and I'll turn on the grill."

As Serena entered the back door to the kitchen, she saw a small suitcase on the floor in the laundry room. How odd. No one was going anywhere this weekend. When she looked up, Mom stood before her.

"Go tell your father I need to talk to him." Mom's face looked weird—sad and angry at the same time.

Something's wrong, Serena thought, as she walked back to the patio. "Mom wants to talk to you, Dad."

Even though Serena knew listening was wrong, she followed Dad as he headed toward the house. He left the door ajar when he entered, and she heard Mom say, "I've been keeping a secret from you for the last several months." Mom cleared her throat. "I've been seeing another woman. We're in love. I'm leaving."

"What?" Dad's voice trailed off. "Wait, Theresa, wait."

Serena rushed out of the garage and peered around the side of the house. Mom carried the small suitcase out to her car, got in, and backed out of the driveway. Serena swiped at the tears running down her face.

Ricky tugged on her arm. "Where's Mom going?" She pushed him aside and walked into the house. Dad sat on the couch, head in his hands. When Serena touched his leg, he looked up. His eyes were red, his cheeks wet with tears.

Serena's vision blurred. She wiped her face on her shirt again and again, but she couldn't stop the tears. Dad opened his arms wide, and she buried herself in his warm embrace.

God understands our sorrow when a loved one announces his or her decision to pursue an LGBTQ+ lifestyle. He feels our pain; He grieves with us. The psalmist gives us the beautiful picture of God leaning close to catch our tears in a bottle. Cry freely. God is crying with you.

Today's Choice: Read Psalms 56 and 57. Envision God's arm around you, comforting you. Envision Him leaning close to catch your tears. Then repeat the psalmist's words as a prayer of thanks to God: "I will thank you, Lord, among all the people. I will sing your praises among the nations. For your unfailing love is as high as the heavens. Your faithfulness reaches to the clouds" (Psalm 57:9–10 NLT).

Reflections:

_____

_____

_____

_____

_____

Desperate and Helpless

But [God] said to me, "My grace is sufficient for you, for my power is made perfect in weakness." Therefore I will boast all the more gladly of my weaknesses, so that the power of Christ may rest upon me.

—2 CORINTHIANS 12:9 (ESV)

Dalton planned to visit PaPa Joe and Gram Alice today. She was in the kitchen frosting Dalton's favorite cake. Joe was mowing the lawn. As he pushed the mower across the last row of grass, Dalton pulled into the driveway in his blue sedan. Joe went over to the car to greet Dalton, but he seemed different, and Joe wondered why his usual happy-go-lucky attitude was missing.

"Hey, PaPa, how are you?"

"Much better, now that you're here," Joe said as he opened Dalton's car door. "Gram's eager to see you too. She's made a chocolate fudge cake."

Alice and Joe always looked forward to seeing their grandchildren, and Dalton had a special place in his grandmother's heart. He'd struggled to fit in with his peers ever since preschool days. As he grew up, they'd encouraged his various interests, tried to help him discover his place and become secure in who he was. But his inner conflict raged on. Alice and Joe prayed daily for God to intervene.

As they ate cake around the kitchen table, Joe said, "You seem gloomy today. What's up?"

"Just things," Dalton murmured, his gaze focused on his plate.

"What things?"

"Mom and Dad don't think my friends are a good influence on me."

"What do you like about them?" Alice asked.

"They don't tease me. They're like family. I feel like I belong for a change."

"Fair enough," Joe said, "but why are your parents concerned?"

"My friends are transgender and told me I was too." Dalton shrugged. "I mean, I guess I am. I'm more comfortable with girls, and I like girls' clothing too. It makes sense to me. I've had so much trouble fitting in, and now I really do."

Joe felt woozy and disoriented, like a soccer ball had just smacked him in the head. He glanced at Alice, and her pale face told him she felt the same way. When she bowed her head, Joe knew she was praying. He sent a silent prayer heavenward too. *Lord, help us. We are desperate. We don't know how to help our grandson or his parents navigate this situation. We need Your wisdom, Your strength.*

God knows how weak, woozy, and disoriented you feel when a loved one announces his or her decision to pursue an LGBTQ+ lifestyle. But God has promised to give you His strength to navigate this journey. His grace is sufficient in all situations—including this one.

> **Today's Choice:** Read 2 Corinthians 12:9–10, then write down why you feel insufficient to handle your current situation. Read each sentence aloud and say, "God's grace is sufficient—more than enough in scope, power, and endurance—to help me do this."

Reflections:

_____

_____

_____

_____

_____

Feeling Forsaken

About the ninth hour Jesus cried out with a loud voice, saying, "Eli, Eli, lama sabachthani?" that is, "My God, My God, why have You forsaken Me?"

—MATTHEW 27:46 (NASB)

The bare branches of the oak tree swayed against the backdrop of a grayish-white sky. Susan sat on the couch with a mug of steaming tea, staring out the window at the swirling snowflakes. Her husband, James, shoveled the sidewalk. A typical winter evening, or so it seemed.

Susan carried her empty mug back to the kitchen and checked on the roast in the oven. Almost done. Time to make the salad. She went to the kitchen door and called out to James, "Dinner's almost ready."

"I'll be right there," he said.

His voice sounded strained. Susan watched her husband trudge across the snow-covered lawn. His expression was grim, his shoulders slumped. Had he pulled a muscle while shoveling?

When James entered the house, he muttered something about the cold as he took off his coat, boots, and gloves. He glanced at Susan.

Something's wrong, she thought. Fear crept up her spine.

"We need to talk," he said.

Her stomach lurched.

"I know what I'm about to tell you will shock you," he said, " but I can't hide the truth about myself anymore. It's been eating me up inside . . . for years." He placed his hands on the table, released a long sigh, then met her gaze. "I love you, but life isn't what it seems. I feel like I'm a woman trapped in a man's body."

Susan gasped.

James shared his plans to leave their home and their marriage as he sought to become what he considered his true self. "This'll be best for both of us. We can move on."

Numbness spread through her body. One phrase circled in her brain: "God, where are You?"

She stumbled out of the kitchen and up the stairs. James' voice chased her: "Susan, Susan!"

How could this be happening? Their marriage had seemed solid, only small bumps along the way. She'd always trusted God, tried to honor Him. Now He felt so far away. Where was He when she needed Him most?

You may feel as though God has forsaken you, but He has not. Jesus suffered separation from God the Father on the cross so that you have permanent access to the Father and the Son.

If you're a believer in Jesus Christ, God is with you, beside you, above you, and inside you. God's presence and watchful care surround you. He invites you to draw near. Open your heart and receive the love, mercy, and comfort He longs to give you.

Today's Choice: Read Matthew 27:45–46 and Psalm 22. Describe the change in the psalmist's attitude between verse 1 and 31. What truths about God enabled him to alter his perspective?

Reflections:

_____

_____

_____

_____

_____

Walk with Me

He heals the brokenhearted and binds up their wounds. The Lord delights in those who fear him, who put their hope in his unfailing love.

—Psalm 147:3, 11

The sun rose at 6:05 a.m. Normally, Tiffany was eager for her morning walk, but today she didn't seem to have the energy to tie her sneakers. "I guess I'll skip my walk today," she said. Her heart was heavy with the news that her cousin Sharon had come out as gay.

Sharon's announcement had shocked Tiffany, but after a few moments of silence, Tiffany had hugged her cousin. "You know I don't think this lifestyle is best for you, but I love you and I'm always here for you." She'd left the restaurant where'd they met for lunch emotionally drained. She needed time alone to digest the heartbreaking news.

Sharon and Tiffany shared so many childhood memories. On summer nights, they'd camped out in the backyard. They'd chased fireflies, told scary stories, and giggled in the darkness until they fell asleep. They took gymnastics classes together and played on the same elementary and high school basketball teams. In high school Tiffany and her boyfriend, Joe, often double-dated with Sharon and her boyfriend, Zeke. Their lives had seemed so normal then.

What went wrong? Sharon had been raised by loving parents in a Christian home. What could have possibly caused Sharon to think she was gay? Nothing made sense.

With a mug of coffee in hand, Tiffany sat on her porch and admired the beautiful sunrise above the mountains. Ripples of pink and orange streaked the sky as darkness faded. "Jesus," she prayed, "why did Sharon start to date a woman? Why didn't I see this coming?"

She then heard a quiet voice speak to her heart: "Child, I know you're disappointed, and your heart is heavy, but you need to put your hope in Me

11

and set aside those questions. I love you. Will you let Me walk beside you in this journey?"

Tiffany whispered, "Yes, Lord, I'll trust You and wait for You to show me the way."

The next day, she awoke early. She still felt emotionally exhausted but decided to take a walk anyway. As she tied her shoes, she smiled. Jesus would walk with her. She prayed, "I'll trust You to walk with me each day and show me how to love Sharon, and I'll trust You to walk with her each day and bring her back to You."

No matter how disappointed we are when a loved one decides to pursue a same-sex relationship, God can heal our broken heart. And He will walk with us on the journey.

Place your hope in His unfailing love.

Today's Choice: If possible, take a walk today in God's beautiful world. As you walk, think about the ways God shows His unfailing love and faithfulness in nature and remind yourself that He also loves you and your loved ones. You may want to write Psalm 147:7–11 on an index card as a reminder of God's faithfulness to both the natural world and to you.

Reflections:

_____

_____

_____

_____

_____

Too Much Loss

Even when the way goes through Death Valley, I'm not afraid when you walk at my side. Your trusty shepherd's crook makes me feel secure.

—Psalm 23:4 (MSG)

When Sarah's mom passed away, she grieved for months. Then, just as she emerged from that dark tunnel, she received a text from her son, Tommy.

"Hey Mom, I'm moving in with my boyfriend, Kevin." Sarah was stunned. She'd raised Tommy right, given him all she had. How could this be true, and where did I go wrong? *If only Mom was here with me*, she thought.

A few weeks passed. Sarah sank deeper into grief over her losses. The unfulfilled dreams of Tommy marrying a woman, having natural grandchildren, and most importantly, Tommy honoring God with his life seemed lost for good. "How can I bear my losses, God?" she prayed.

No answer came. Pain filled her heart and all her hope evaporated.

Sarah lost her appetite for food and life. Some days she lay in bed for hours, a blanket pulled over her head. Friends left messages on her phone: praying for you; please call me. But Sarah didn't have the energy to return their calls.

"Where are You, God?" she asked.

This time, though, a small still voice answered, "I'm right here by your side."

She gasped. Had God spoken to her, or was it her imagination?

The following day, someone knocked on her door as Sarah lay on the couch. A familiar voice said, "Sarah, it's Janey. I've been trying to reach out to you. Please let me in."

Sarah didn't respond. A few minutes later, Janey tapped on the living room window. "Please let me in. I'm worried about you."

Sarah eased off the couch, trudged to the door, and opened it.

Janey gave Sarah a hug and held her tight. Pulling back, she said, "Oh Sarah, I'm so sorry for all you're going through. I know your mom's loss was difficult, then when I received your text about Tommy, I didn't know how to respond. Please forgive me for not reaching out sooner."

Sarah motioned for Janey to come in. Her heart felt lighter. Why had she waited so long to connect with a friend?

The urge to hide and isolate is strong when we're in pain. But just as we need to reach out to God in these times, we need to allow friends to share our burden. As the psalmist says, God's beauty and love chase after us every day (v. 6 MSG), and often He sends His love through a human friend.

Today's Choice: Read Psalm 23 in *The Message* or in another modern version. What stands out to you in this familiar psalm? How is God's beauty and love chasing after you today?

Reflections:

_____

_____

_____

_____

_____

Are You Hiding from Me, God?

How long, O Lord? Will you forget me forever?
How long will you hide your face from me?

—PSALM 13:1 (ESV)

Russ and Sondra married in their mid-twenties. God blessed them with three children—Leaf, Mitchell, and Hailey. For years, life sailed along smoothly. But during Leaf's freshman year in college and Mitchell's senior year in high school, the boys' attitudes changed. They rebelled against family rules and refused to attend church. Both claimed they no longer believed in God.

One day when Sondra came home from work, Hailey was unusually quiet. "Hailey, what's going on?"

No answer. Sondra tried again. "Hailey, are you okay?" Then she noticed her daughter had been crying. "Please tell me what's wrong."

"Oh Mom, I don't know why the boys use me as the go-between to give bad news to you and Dad."

"It's okay." Sondra sat on the couch next to Hailey. "You'll feel better if you just say whatever it is."

"After dinner last night, I went out to say goodbye to Leaf before he headed back to his dorm room. He said he and Mitchell wanted to tell me something, that they'd held off as long as they could, but it was time."

"Time for what?"

"Leaf said he's bisexual, but he's more attracted to boys than girls. Then he glanced over at Mitchell and said, 'See that's not so hard to tell her.' Mitchell didn't say anything at first, but Leaf kept pressuring him."

Hailey bit her lower lip. "Mitchell finally said, 'I'm like Leaf in a way. I'd rather date men. Never had luck with girls anyway. I've been dating Joseph since eleventh grade, and I'd like you to meet him.'"

Sondra's eyes filled with tears, and her heart thumped hard against her chest. How could her family's world be turned upside down like this?

When Russ came home that evening, Sondra and Hailey told him the news. For the first time it seemed like God was hiding from him—unaware or maybe even uninterested in this family catastrophe. Russ knew the news didn't surprise God, but why hadn't He revealed what was going on? Shame crept into Russ's heart. Where did he go wrong as a father? What had he done or not done to drive his sons into this lifestyle? "Oh, Lord," he prayed, "how we need You!"

The shock of a loved one's decision to pursue a same-sex relationship is devastating, but the news doesn't mean God is hiding from you. In fact, He wants to draw closer to you on this journey. Ask Him for help, as Russ did. Converse with God—tell Him everything that's on your heart and listen for His voice. He will respond.

Today's Choice: Read Psalm 13. How is David's attitude in verses 3–6 different from his attitude in verses 1–2? What do you think changed his perspective? How can you follow David's example?

Reflections:

_____

_____

_____

_____

_____

Living in Shame

Fear not; you will no longer live in shame.
Do not be afraid; there is no more disgrace for you.

—Isaiah 54:4 (NLT)

The alarm clock rang at 6:00 a.m. "I don't like Monday's," Christy grumbled as she rolled out of bed.

When she walked into the kitchen, Peter had already put his English muffin in the toaster and a mug of yesterday's coffee in the microwave. Grabbing both, he nodded goodbye and left. The growing tension in their marriage concerned her, but when she attempted to speak with Peter about the friction, they generally ended up arguing about something else.

That afternoon as she drove home from work, she thought she recognized Peter's truck parked at her favorite restaurant. Was Peter buying her a gift certificate or setting up a surprise dinner date? Maybe he wanted to make amends for last night's argument. She smiled, then decided to swing by the grocery store and buy steak for dinner.

Dinner was just about ready when Peter came home. "Hi, honey," she said. "I made your favorite tonight—steak and fried potatoes."

"Oh, that's nice." He sidestepped her and headed for the family room.

"Hey," she called after him. "I saw your truck at Olivia's Restaurant."

"What?" Peter turned, his face pale.

"Umm . . . you'd better sit down," he said and motioned her toward a chair. "I'm not sure how to tell you this . . . Oh gosh . . . how . . . I don't want to hurt you." He ran his fingers through his hair. "You're a wonderful person. But it's unfair to both of us for me to stay silent any longer. I've been meeting up with Matt—an old friend from high school I reconnected with on Facebook. I love him, Christy, and I'm moving in with him next week."

"What? When . . . how . . ." She burst into tears. "Never mind, I don't want to know." She shoved her chair back from the table and ran upstairs.

She flung herself on the bed and let the storm of tears loose. Shame washed over her. What was wrong with her? How could Peter betray her with another man? This is the worst thing that can happen to a wife. How could she face anyone—man or woman? I cannot tell anyone about this. It's too shameful. What will they think of me?

Heaping shame on yourself for your spouse's or loved one's sin is poisonous. Don't believe the Enemy's lies. You are not at fault. As a child of God, redeemed by the blood of Jesus, you are forever free from shame. Allow His cleansing love to flow over you.

Today's Choice: Read Isaiah 54:4–8. Although these words were originally written for the nation of Israel, they are also applicable to us. Ask God to embrace you with His eternal, unchanging love and compassion today. Ask Him to remove any shame and fill you with a renewed sense of worth and beauty.

Reflections:

_____

_____

_____

_____

_____

Unspeakable Pain

Whoever dwells in the shelter of the Most High will rest in the shadow of the Almighty. I will say of the Lord, "He is my refuge and my fortress, my God, in whom I trust."

—Psalm 91:1–2

Terri hummed an upbeat tune as she changed the sheets on her son Shawn's bed. She was so thankful he'd chosen to come home for Spring Break instead of heading to the beach with friends.

When she heard a car pull into the driveway, she looked out the window. Shawn. As she reached the front door, Shawn opened it. "Hi, Mom."

Terri stood speechless. Her gaze moved from his ponytail to his black T-shirt and leather pants. His long fingernails were covered with bright red polish. Her heart pounded.

"I know this is a surprise, Mom, but this is who I really am. Please call me Michelle." Her mind whirled. Shawn had always struggled with self-esteem, and he'd been devastated when his girlfriend broke up with him. But she never imagined this.

"I need to sit down," she squeaked and headed to the kitchen.

A few minutes later, Terri's husband, Mickey, hollered from the front hallway. "Hey, I see Shawn's car is here." He stopped in the kitchen doorway. "What's going on here, Shawn?"

"This is who I really am."

"What are you talking about? This is not who you are, son."

"Yes, it is. In psychology class, I learned about how traditional stereotypes can pressure us into hiding who we truly are. Several of my classmates figured out they were gay or bisexual, and six of us decided we were really transgender people trying to live in a construct world."

"Son, we need to talk further about this. You just came home. We haven't had a chance to grasp all you're saying."

"Well, Dad, this is the way it is." Shawn stood. "Maybe I should stay over at Tim's house until you can accept me as I am."

"No, son, wait," Mickey called out. Shawn kept walking.

Terri pushed her chair away from the table, hurried upstairs to the master bedroom, and locked the door. She felt as if her chest was bursting.

Someone jiggled the door handle. "Terri, darling," Mickey said, "I'm here for you. I'm not going anywhere. We need each other right now, and we need God."

When what we consider normal is stripped from us, we feel abandoned, bewildered, adrift. But God is our refuge, our safe place. In His presence we can find rest—calm, comfort, balance. He brings others alongside us too. Let Him calm you today. Let Him be your safe place.

Today's Choice: Read Psalm 91, then list on an index card or sticky note the "I will" promises in verses 14–16. Put that list where you'll see it every day.

Reflections:

_____

_____

_____

_____

_____

When Others Judge You

Jesus said, *"Do not judge or you too will be judged. For in the same way you judge others, you will be judged, and with the measure you use, it will be measured to you."*

—MATTHEW 7:1–2

Your heartbeat quickens and your stomach flip-flops as you sit in the church pew next to an acquaintance or at a family member's dining room table. Even if they greet you with a smile, you may wonder if they're judging you because your loved one came out LGBTQ+. You wonder what conclusions that person has drawn about your parenting style or your marriage. What did you do wrong to drive your loved one into the LGBTQ+ lifestyle?

God isn't surprised by our human tendency to judge one another harshly. If someone is judging you or your circumstances, you may want to lash out at that person or defend yourself. But resist that urge. Yes, the other person's judgmental attitude hurts you and offends God, but He doesn't give us a pass on this matter just because we're in pain.

First, remember that God isn't judging you. He doesn't condemn you for your loved one's choices. His arms of love are open to you, and He wants to walk alongside you in this journey.

Second, keep in mind that God has work to do in your life just as He has work to do in other people's lives. Jesus said, "How can you say to your brother, 'Let me take the speck out of your eye,' when all the time there is a plank in your own eye?" (Matthew 7:4). That's not what we want to hear when others have judged us unfairly, but we need to guard our own heart against the cancer of a judgmental spirit and back away from the temptation to judge the one who is judging us!

Instead, allow God time to deal with that person in His time and in His way. He alone is the one righteous judge. He says, "I choose the appointed time; it is I who judge with equity" (Psalm 75:2). And, as hard as it may be to accept, God loves the person who's judging you and wants to cultivate a nonjudgmental spirit in their heart too. He can give you the strength to "pray for those who persecute you"—for those who speak unkindly, spread rumors, or draw false conclusions about you or your situation (Matthew 5:44).

If others are judging you, pray for them and ask God to bless them until you mean it so bitterness doesn't take over. If you're judging others because of what they've said to you or others about your circumstances, pray for them and ask God to bless them until you mean it.

He's in the heart transformation business. He can change their heart and yours.

Today's Choice: Read Matthew 7:1–5 and 1 Corinthians 4:3–5. What is God saying to you about how to treat those who judge you in these passages?

Reflections:

_____

_____

_____

_____

_____

Undying Love

And so we know and rely on the love God has for us. God is love.
Whoever lives in love lives in God, and God in them.

—1 JOHN 4:16

J im knew something was wrong when he read the Subject line in his younger brother's email: "We need to talk."

Jim replied, "Sure, Lucas. Want to come over and shoot a few baskets early tomorrow morning? We could grab a late breakfast afterward."

"See you at 7:00," Lucas responded.

Throughout the day, Jim thought about his brother's email. Lucas traveled a lot. Were he and Hannah having marriage problems? Or maybe their sixteen-year-old twins, Jason and Madison, were struggling with typical high school stuff.

When Lucas pulled into the driveway the next morning, Jim walked out to meet him. He looked exhausted.

"Jim," Lucas said, "I don't have the energy to play ball. Got some coffee brewing?"

"Come on in. Tabitha's not here. On her way to Nashville to visit a friend."

Seated at the kitchen table with a mug of coffee, Jim said, "Lucas, I've been praying for you and Hannah ever since I got your email. Don't know what's up, but I'm here for you."

"This is hard." Lucas shook his head. "Maddie announced that she's really Mason, not Madison."

"What?"

"She says she's never felt like a girl—not even when she was young." Lucas stood and paced. "We don't know what to do. Heck, I can't even think straight at work. My boss knows something's up, but I can't tell him. Everyone so liberal there, they probably think it's okay anyway. Hannah's a mess too. All I do is hold her when she cries."

"You're doing the right thing, Lucas—holding her, I mean." An awkward silence followed, then Jim said, "What about Jason?"

Lucas's voice trembled. "Maddie wants him to call her a brother and treat her like a boy, but Jason won't do it." Lucas ran his hands through his hair. "The whole thing's crazy—feels like I've landed on some weird planet with no way to return to earth. The school counselor called Hannah last Tuesday and suggested we attend a PFlag support group." He clenched his jaw. "We won't go. They only encourage parents to accept their child as a transgender. We'd rather seek support from other families who know God."

"Let Tabitha and me walk this journey with you. Let's see what God's Word has for us. That's where we'll find understanding, truth, and grace."

Lucas gave Jim a shaky smile. "Thanks, brother. I knew I could count on you to meet us where we are."

"God's undying love for us," Jim said. "That's what will get us through."

> **Today's Choice:** Read 1 John 4:9–19. What does this passage teach us about the love of God? How do we know His love remains constant no matter what we're going through?

Reflections:

_____

_____

_____

_____

_____

An Unforgettable Holiday

In whose case the god of this world has blinded the minds of the unbelieving so that they might not see the light of the gospel of the glory of Christ, who is the image of God.

—2 Corinthians 4:4 (NASB)

For Tom, the holiday season meant big family gatherings, full of fun and delicious food. Aunt Judy made the best stuffing, Grandma Pat baked the perfect pies, and Grandpa Ron cooked the most tender turkey imaginable. Tom and his cousins gathered in a large room where puzzles were laid out on tables, and younger children played board games on the floor.

On one holiday, a family member arrived later than usual. Grandpa Ron's voice sounded odd when he answered the door. "Tony? Is that you, Tony?"

Why would Grandpa be asking if the person was Uncle Tony, Tom wondered. Surely, he knew his own son.

A voice answered, "Of course it's me, Dad."

Grandpa Ron said nothing. Moments later, Tom heard some gasps in the kitchen. Aunt Judy asked, "Is this a bad joke?" Tom's dad said, "What's going on, Tony?" Tom whispered to his cousin Jodi, "Whatever's going on out there, I want no part of it." She nodded.

Uncle Stephen's voice rose above the others. "Tony, what's this about?"

"I know this is a surprise to you all, but I thought it'd be best to show up today as who I am. I'm tired of living a lie. I'm a woman, and I ask you to accept me as Theresa."

Oh no! Tom thought. Jodi's eyes widened. Tom turned up the TV volume, hoping to distract his younger cousins. Then he and Jodi moved the puzzle table closer to the door so they could hear the adults.

In the kitchen, Aunt Judy asked everyone to sit down. Some voices sounded angry, others confused, but most sounded sad.

Anger bubbled up inside Tom. Leaning over the table, he whispered to Jodi, "Does he think we're going to call him Aunt Theresa? What right does he have to come and just blow up our holiday like this?"

Jodi looked over at the two younger cousins playing Monopoly and whispered, "This will confuse Bobby and Derek more than us. They're Uncle Tony's favorites. They look up to him."

Tom shook his head. How could Uncle Tony act this way? It made no sense.

Loved ones who identify as LGBTQ+ rarely consider how their decision will impact the rest of the family. Satan has blinded them to their foolishness and filled their minds with lies about the effects of their decision. Allow the younger members of your family to express their feelings openly about the LGBTQ+ loved one, and guide them toward a godly, yet loving attitude.

Today's Choice: Read 2 Corinthians 4:4–6, 16–18. How can you shine the light of Jesus into your family as you all walk the journey of a loved one identifying as LGBTQ+? What unseen (eternal) truths can you fix your eyes on?

Reflections:

_____

_____

_____

_____

_____

Can This Wound Be Healed?

He breaks me with wound upon wound. He runs at me like a warrior.

—Job 16:14 (NKJV)

As a nurse, Nancy marveled over the human body's the ability to heal, and she loved caring for others. She and her husband, Phil, had a strong marriage and thanked God for their two daughters, Jacki and Jill.

Then one day Jacki came for a visit and announced she was moving in with a woman she met online, several states away. Nancy gasped for air, as if her windpipe had been crushed.

"What are you talking about?" Phil said. "You met this woman online, had a few face-to-face conversations, and now you're moving in with her? Please stop me if I'm misunderstanding you."

"I know you don't approve, and to be honest I don't care. We've had an online relationship for six months, and we're ready to take the next step. Mia's ten years older than I am, divorced with three children." Jacki smiled. "Look at this way—you've just become grandparents."

Thoughts bounced around like a tennis ball in Nancy's head. She cared for people all the time, but she was clueless about caring for her family in this situation.

"You try to paint this as a pretty picture by saying we'll be grandparents?" Phil's voice shook. "Have you considered what Mia's children will think of their mom sharing a bed with another woman? I can't believe you thought we'd celebrate this with you."

Phil paced the floor, then turned to Jacki. "Does Jill know?"

"I told her last week. She's not in favor of my decision either and hasn't spoke to me since I told her. I know she needs some space, but I hope she'll visit Mia and me when she's ready."

Nancy found her voice. "I love you, Jacki, but I cannot in good conscience bless your decision. I won't get into the biblical reasons. You know why we believe it's morally wrong. With three children in the mix, this will impact all of us in ways none of us can imagine." She took a deep breath. "This isn't all about you. You've shaken me, Dad, and Jill. I can barely breath."

When Jacki left, Nancy felt as if a surgeon had cut her heart into pieces and couldn't put it together again. She collapsed on the couch, trying to stop the pain by wrapping her arms tightly around her chest. How could this wound ever heal?

Your wounds may feel incurable today, but God is able to bring healing to you and your family. Talk to Him about your pain. Allow Him to comfort you.

Today's Choice: Read Job 16:12–22. In what ways do you identify with Job's pain? In verse 21, he asks for an advocate. Who is our advocate according to 1 Timothy 2:5? What do you want Jesus to say to God the Father on your behalf today?

Reflections:

_____

_____

_____

_____

_____

God Isn't Finished

And we know that in all things God works for the good of those who love him,
who have been called according to his purpose.

—ROMANS 8:28

When Roy proposed to Janet, she said, "Yes, of course I'll marry you. We'll be together for life."

Three years into their marriage, Joey was born, then Alex, and lastly Jennifer. The years passed quickly. Before they knew it, their kids were adults. Jennifer, Joey, and his wife, Samantha, lived in Kentucky near Roy and Janet. To take a good-paying job after college, Alex had moved to California. All seemed well.

Then one day Alex called to arrange a family FaceTime. A heaviness settled in Roy's heart. Why did Alex's voice sound so strange?

On Sunday night, the Kentucky family members gathered for a barbecue. After they ate, Roy pulled out the iPad to call Alex. The rest of the family crowded around the screen.

"Hey, thanks everyone for meeting with me tonight," Alex said. "I have some news and, to be honest, it'll be easier if I say it just once. A lot has happened since I relocated to California, and I've found a piece of me that was missing." He took a deep breath. "I'm really a woman, and I've changed my name to Alexandra."

Roy's heart pounded like a jackhammer in the silence.

"I know this is hard, but I'd like you to call me your daughter or sister, and use female pronouns. If you love me, you'll do this for me. I hope you understand—after all, we are family."

The despair and shock Roy felt was mirrored in the faces of the other family members. Eyes wide, they looked from one to another. Tears fell. No words came. Finally, Roy tapped into enough strength to say, "Alex, we love you."

In the following weeks, Janet pushed Roy toward doing what Alex requested. "You must call him Alexandra. We can't lose him." Anger blazed in her eyes. "I won't deny him and lose my child."

Roy resisted. A year later, Janet announced she was leaving unless he accepted their daughter Alexandra. When Roy continued to reject Janet's manipulative tactics, she left, declaring she wouldn't return unless he changed his mind.

Had Roy lost it all? No. He clings to the One who loves him unconditionally. He says, "I don't know what tomorrow holds, but I have faith that God is with me and that He hears my prayers for Alex, for Janet, and for my marriage and family to be restored."

Like Roy, you can cling to the promise of Romans 8:28. God can bring good out of every situation and restore what has been lost.

> **Today's Choice:** Read Romans 8:28–31. Instead of thinking about all that could go wrong in your present circumstances, make a list of what good God could bring out of this situation, then thank Him for His unchanging, unconditional love that will uphold you until that good comes to pass.

Reflections:

_____

_____

_____

_____

_____

Happiness Turned to Numbness

You will keep in perfect peace those whose minds are steadfast, because they trust in you. Trust in the Lord forever, for the Lord, the Lord himself is the Rock eternal.

—Isaiah 26:3–4

When Stephen came home from work, he greeted his wife, Jan, and sat in the rocker next to her on the front porch. "You look pretty cheerful," he said. "You must've had a great day at work."

"It was a pretty good day," she said, but I'm most happy about the message I got from Noah today.

He leaned toward her. "What's going on?"

"He's coming home next weekend, has someone he wants us to meet."

"I think he mentioned a Joy a while back. Maybe it's her."

Jan smiled. "Whoever she is, I'm sure we'll love her as much as he does."

That Saturday, Stephen and Jan looked at each other with raised eyebrows as they watched Noah and another young man get out of the car.

Once inside, Noah and his parents hugged one another. Then Noah said, "Mom, Dad, I want you meet Alan."

Jan hid her disappointment but greeted Alan with a smile. "Good to meet you. Supper's ready. Let's go sit down."

During dinner, Stephen noticed Alan's hand rested on Stephen's thigh. He tried to act nonchalant, but Jan noticed his facial expression.

"What's wrong, Stephen?" she said. "You look like you swallowed a frog."

Noah placed both his hands on the table and met his father's eyes. "Mom and Dad, Alan and I need to talk to you."

Jan's throat tightened. "Sure, son," she squeaked. "What's going on?"

"I know this is going to surprise you," Noah said, "but the secret is killing me. Alan and I are a couple."

Jan felt dizzy, and her heartbeat quickened. She clamped a hand over her mouth to stop herself from screaming.

Perhaps you've been blindsided by a similar announcement from a loved one. No matter how hard we try, we can't prepare ourselves for all the what-ifs in life, but we can prepare ourselves to turn to the One who will catch us when we can't catch our breath.

If you push down worries or allow them free rein, you'll become over-burdened with stress that can jeopardize your mental, physical, and spiritual health.

What is the "perfect peace" God promises to give? The calmness of heart and mind that Jesus, your shepherd, places inside you. It is a supernatural sense of well-being that comes from meditating on His promises and relinquishing control of the situation to Him.

Put your trust in Jesus, the Eternal Rock. He will support you through this numbness and guide you into happiness again.

Today's Choice: Pray the promises of Isaiah 26:3–4 and 32:17–18 back to God. Tell Him that you trust Him to fulfill these promises for you and for your LGBTQ+ loved one.

Reflections:

_____

_____

_____

_____

_____

Is Death the Better Choice?

"Now, Lord, take away my life, for it is better for me to die than to live."

—Jonah 4:3

When Dad left our family to live as Becky, Mom sank into depression. My siblings struggled with deep grief. And me? Darkness engulfed me. I wanted to stay in bed and pull the covers over my head so I didn't have to face reality. Choosing death seemed easier than living with the facts: my dad was attempting the impossible—become a woman.

I tried to be strong for my mom and younger siblings, yet I was barely surviving. I pushed Dad's struggle with same-sex attraction and his desire to be female into a dark corner of my soul. But God forced me bring all that pain to the surface and deal with it many years later.

After Dad's passing, I was asked to clean out his home. In his bedroom closet and drawers, I sorted through his female clothing. At times, the process became overwhelming. The room next to his bedroom was filled with nearly one hundred dolls, each a symbol of his fantasy world.

I also found letters he'd written to other men. I could barely hold them steady. My heart pounded as I read them. Some letters were from other men living as gay; others were from men adapting to a female role.

Feelings of darkness and heaviness once again overwhelmed me. My head ached; my stomach churned. I couldn't absorb any more pain or grief that day.

Mom was with me at Dad's house, trying to help. I found her in another room and said, "We've done enough today. I have a headache and need to rest." When I reached my brother's home, I collapsed. Why couldn't God have taken me home to heaven without knowing the horrible truth about Dad?

I battled anger, bitterness, and despair. Would I cling to Jesus or remain in the darkness? I prayed, "Dear God, I need Your help. I can't go through

Dad's house and belongings without You. I need Your strength. In Jesus' name, amen."

After a good night's sleep, I shared the letters with my brother the next morning. My mom and sister worked with me at the house. I handed my sister the box of letters. "Please put these aside for me," confident God would show me what to do with them later.

On several occasions, I've thought dying might be easier than living. You may feel that way today. But God isn't finished with me, and He isn't finished with you. He has work for us to do. Will you trust Him? He is faithful.

Today's Choice: Read Jonah's words in Jonah 4:1–3. How could his prayer of desperation in 2:1–9 have helped him overcome his despair in chapter 4? What can you glean from his prayer that can help you today?

Reflections:

_____

_____

_____

_____

_____

Unshakable Guilt

*That the creation itself will be set free from its bondage to corruption
and obtain the freedom of the glory of the children of God.*

—Romans 8:21 (ESV)

From his front yard, Ron watched the neighbor, Tom, toss a baseball back and forth with his son, Shawn. Ron chuckled when Tom, attempting to reach the ball that soared high above his head, landed on the ground.

He sighed. He'd been so busy when Mitchell was that age. Work had consumed his weekdays and weekends. At that time, Ron figured the more overtime the better. He and his wife, Renee, wanted the extra money for family vacations, Mitchell's college fund, and their retirement. Surely, Renee and Mitchell had understood why he'd missed so many meals, school concerts, and church services. After all, being a police officer was important.

A gloominess settled in his soul, and he turned back toward the house. Go inside. Forget about Tom and Shawn. Mitchell had never wanted to play catch anyway. He'd always been more interested in the arts—piano lessons, jazz band, and drama club.

Guilt welled up. How could I have been so clueless, so stupid? Maybe if I'd spent more time with Mitchell, he wouldn't be gay. Why didn't I support his love for music? Why did I choose overtime instead of attending his concerts and plays?

"Hey, Ron, what's wrong?" He looked up. Renee stood on the front porch, concern etched on her face.

"Why did I work so much when Mitchell was young?" He slung an arm around his wife's shoulder as they walked into the house. "If I hadn't worked so much, maybe Mitchell wouldn't have chosen a gay lifestyle. I should've known how important it was to spend time with him. I sure treasured time with my dad."

He turned and faced Renee, his voice thick with emotion. "I kept telling myself, 'Mitchell's fine. One more weekend of overtime, then I'll spend more time with him.' But that one more weekend turned into many, many more."

"All parents make mistakes." She slid her arms around his waist. "Tell Mitchell how you feel. Admit that you aren't a perfect dad, that you're sorry you missed so many of his school activities." She wiped a tear from Ron's cheek. "He's stopping by Monday to grab a few of his old music books. Why don't you ask about his band, about the songs he writes?"

Ron smiled. "You're right. I've got to try."

"Guilt will destroy us if we allow it to. It keeps us bound to past mistakes. God has freed us from that. Let's move forward."

Today's Choice: Read Romans 8:18–27. What parenting mistakes are keeping you bound to your past? According to verses 26–27, what is the Holy Spirit's role in releasing us from bondage and filling us with hope? What do you need to release to Him?

Reflections:

_____

_____

_____

_____

_____

Is Anything Too Hard for God?

"For nothing is impossible with God."

—LUKE 1:37 (NLT)

W hen I was fifteen, a friend named Lauren told me, "To show God that I trust Him to heal my eyesight, I'm not going to wear glasses anymore." A new Christian myself, I wasn't sure what to think about her act of faith.

As time passed, I wondered why God didn't heal Lauren's vision. Was it too difficult for Him to do? No, but for some reason He chose not to improve her eyesight. Still, I admired her faith and her ability to accept God's answer even though she wanted a different outcome.

Sometimes when we ask God to do something that seems to be aligned with His will, we wonder why He doesn't give us what we desire. After all, can't He just say, "Let it be so," and automatically His words become reality?

When young Mary asked how she could become pregnant since she was a virgin, the angel Gabriel reminded her, "Nothing is impossible with God" (Luke 1:37 NLT). Jesus said the same thing to the disciples about salvation: "With man this is impossible, but with God all things are possible" (Matthew 19:26).

So if God can do all things, why doesn't He? He's more interested in our character than in our comfort. We learn how to persevere and become steadfast in our faith through our circumstances. He calls us to believe His promises wholeheartedly, including the promise that He is working all things together for our good and His glory, even the hard things—maybe especially the hard things.

Your journey is about faith building—not just for you but also for the loved one you are praying on behalf of and begging God to bring home. A friend once said, "I want my loved one to come home to God before he returns to us. That is more important to me than instantly having my pain removed."

God loves to send help, but He provides that help at the most opportune time in accordance with His plan for everyone, not just His plan for you or me. Like Lauren, we need to accept the answer God gives today, believing that it's the best possible answer He could give at this time.

Satan wants us to turn away from God in anger when He says no. But instead, we can choose to love Him enough and trust Him enough to believe that today's no may be part of His plan to build our faith and our loved one's faith in the One Healer who can do all things.

Today's Choice: Read Luke 1:26–38. What was incomprehensible and terrifying about Mary's situation? What was her response to Gabriel's statement that God could do anything? What does that show about Mary's faith? How can you follow her example?

Reflections:

_____

_____

_____

_____

_____

Filled with Anger

In your anger do not sin: Do not let the sun go down while you are still angry,
and do not give the devil a foothold.

—Ephesians 4:26–27

Mary Jo tried to concentrate on the road, but fear rose within her. She gripped the steering wheel tighter. What could have upset her sister Nancy so much? Her voice sounded desperate on the phone. Had something happened to her husband, Jake, or one of her kids?

She pulled into her sister's driveway behind her brother-in-law's truck, hurried up the front steps, then opened the front door. "Nancy, it's me. Where are you?"

Jake's voice drifted into the hallway. She headed toward the kitchen. When she entered, Jake was embracing Nancy, rubbing her back and whispering in her ear.

"Jake, what's going on?"

"I'm so glad you came. Nancy needs you."

"Are Ally and Jeff okay?"

Jake closed his eyes and sighed. "Not really. Nancy was making our summer vacation reservations online, and a Facebook window opened. When she clicked on Jeff's page, a number of pictures came up." He swallowed. "Jeff was dressed as a girl. At first, she thought it was a joke, but there were many other pictures of him with gay couples and transgenders. In one photo, Jeff was holding hands with his friend James."

"Oh my." Not knowing what else to do, Mary Jo hugged both Nancy and Jake.

"There's more," Nancy squeaked.

"Ally walked in while Jeff's Facebook page was up and confirmed that Jeff was using a female identity outside the home. But then she said, 'Lighten up,

Mom. There's nothing wrong with Jeff being a female or having a relationship with James. He has to embrace who he really is.'"

"I can't believe Ally would say such a ridiculous thing—or that Jeff would do something like that. You raised them right. How could they do this to you?"

Back at home, Mary Jo paced the living room. Anger boiled inside her—for the hurt her nephew and niece had caused. How could those two teens do this to their loving parents? She felt like someone had poured boiling water down her throat. She couldn't sleep, and she didn't want to eat.

"Help me, Lord. I'm filled with anger. Nancy and Jake are hurting so badly, and I can't stop the pain."

When life blindsides us, anger is a natural response. But God asks us to turn our anger over to Him so it doesn't become rage or bitterness the devil can use to drive us away from God. God already knows you're angry. Vent your anger, then let Him speak peace to your soul.

Today's Choice: Read Ephesians 4:25–32. What counsel is given in this passage about words? What steps can we take that will help us get rid of anger and bitterness?

Reflections:

_____

_____

_____

_____

_____

Consumed with Worry

Don't worry about anything; instead, pray about everything. Tell God what you need, and thank him for all he has done. Then you will experience God's peace, which exceeds anything we can understand. His peace will guard your hearts and mind as you live in Christ Jesus.

—Philippians 4:6–7 (NLT)

Nadine sighed, wadded tissue in hand. Why had her only son, Bruce, strayed so far from God?

A knock at the door signaled her friend Jodi's arrival, but Nadine didn't have the energy to get off the couch. She picked up her phone and texted Jodi. "Door's unlocked."

Jodi walked into Nadine's family room. "Hey, what's going on—why didn't you . . ."

Nadine motioned Jodi over to the couch. "I . . . I . . ."

"I'm here for you, friend." Jodie sat and wrapped her arm around Nadine's shoulders.

Could Jodi be there for her? Nadine wondered. She seemed to have the perfect life—a loving husband, successful adult children, financial security. What could she know about my pain?

Nadine had been hiding a painful secret from her friend, but maybe it was time to share it. "I haven't been honest with you about Bruce. He and his family aren't doing well . . . not at all." She let the tears fall. "I've been so full of grief and worry for them . . . I didn't want to tell you. Your kids are doing so well."

"We've been through tough times with our children too. Remember Alex's drug problem during high school and John's run-in with the police?" She patted Jodi's hand. "Just tell me."

Nadine took a deep breath. "Bruce is leaving Cheri and the kids. The worst part is that he believes he's a woman. He's already begun hormone therapy, and Cheri said it's become even more difficult because the hormones are producing physical changes."

41

She stood and paced the room. "Why doesn't see what he's giving up? I can't stop worrying. I can't sleep, can't eat, and I feel dead inside. What's Bruce doing to himself? I've done some online reading, and studies show the mental, physical, and emotional damage these hormones can do. He's always been so careful and smart, but now he's tossed all common sense out the window." Her voice shook with anger. "How could God do this to me? I tried so hard to bring Bruce up right after his father died."

A long silence followed. Finally, Jodi said, "I don't have words to take your worries away, and I don't know much about this type of brokenness, but I'll stand with you. I'm your friend, and I care deeply for you. May I pray over you and ask God to surround you with His peace right now?"

Worry cannot mend brokenness or ease heartbreak. Only God's peace can protect us and heal us. Are you willing to give your worries to Him?

Today's Choice: Read Philippians 4:6–9. What are you worrying about today? Write each worry on a slip of paper, then put the slips of paper in a fireproof dish and burn them. Let that act represent your willingness to hand your worries to God. Ask Him to fill you with His peace.

Reflections:

_____

_____

_____

_____

_____

Alone with Abba

The Spirit you received brought about your adoption to sonship.
And by him we cry, "Abba, Father."

—ROMANS 8:15

When Alicia heard of her daughter Teresa's sexual choices, she became distraught. Teresa's situation seemed out of control as she moved from one lover to another, seeking to satisfy her craving to emotionally connect with other women.

Late one night, Alicia broke down. She lay on the cold ceramic kitchen floor weeping so hard that she gasped for breath. When her tears subsided, she lashed out at God: "Why did You allow this to happen? I've always sought Your ways and done what You've asked, even when it was painful. But this is too cruel. I can't bear it. Please take this away from me."

Jesus' words in Mark 14:36 came to mind: "*Abba*, Father ... everything is possible for you. Take this cup from me." Alicia then realized she couldn't say the rest of the verse honestly: "yet not what I will, but what you will."

For several hours, she wrestled with God—yelling, sobbing, grieving. Exhausted, she finally quieted down. Then she heard His voice: "Climb into My lap and be still."

In His hour of anguish, Jesus showed us that the Almighty God is also our "*Abba*, Father." *Abba* means daddy—the name a young Jewish child uses for a loving father. Our Abba knows what we need before we ask Him (Matthew 6:8). And sometimes we need to climb into His lap and allow Him to embrace us, calm us.

Our image of God will either draw us closer or drive us away from Him in difficult times. He wants us to curl up in His lap and release our cares to Him. When we focus on our problems, we are basically telling God, "I need to take care of this. I'm in control. I need to fix this."

God is our helper and friend, but if we don't turn toward Him and surrender to Him, we cannot experience His comfort or His power. When we distance ourselves from Him, we're vulnerable to stress, worry, frustration, anger, and pain. And what a pity. Jesus suffered a horrific death so we can draw near to our Abba.

As Alicia continued to communicate with God about Teresa, she learned to release her worries and stress to Him. Most importantly, she learned to climb into His lap and allow Him to fill her with His peace and love. Eventually, she was able to say, "If it's not Your will to take this cup away from me, help me to accept it."

Today's Choice: What aspects of your situation are you unable to yield to God? Read Romans 8:15–17 and 26–27. Ask the Holy Spirit to intercede for you and give you the desire to yield to your Abba.

Reflections:

_____

_____

_____

_____

_____

A Father's Heart

As a father has compassion on his children,
so the Lord has compassion on those who fear him.

—Psalm 103:13

Like many young boys, Sam wanted to be just like his dad, Richard, when he grew up. If neighbors had a leaky roof or a broken-down car, they called his dad. Kind and outgoing, Richard responded with a smile to even the angriest person. Others often came to him for advice and counsel; Richard listened and prayed but never condemned.

As an adult, Sam followed his dad's example and hoped his son, Owen, would follow his example too. Isn't that every dad's dream?

Near Owen's seventeenth birthday, though, Sam found porn magazines filled with naked men stashed in the trunk of Owen's car. Where did this come from? Sam didn't have a clue, at least not yet.

A few years later, Owen began to own the idea he was born gay. Sam and Owen talked about it, but the conversation always ended poorly. Owen kept saying, "That's how my LGBTQ+ friends said you'd respond. If you were a good dad, you'd support my decision to live as an actively gay man."

After Owen moved out of his parents' house, one of his friends told Sam that an older cousin had sexually molested Owen when he was eleven years old. Shame washed over Sam. Why hadn't he been there to rescue his son from a crime that had stolen so much from him?

When his car needs repair, Owen calls Sam for help, and he visits occasionally. Owen gives his dad a lot of silent stares, as if there are words he wishes to say but can't speak them. Their visits seem like a bizarre game of charades—both pretending that everything is okay even though nothing is right between them.

At times, Sam wishes that the older cousin who assaulted Owen would die in some horrible way. Then God reminds him that hurt people hurt people. The grace Sam's dad extended to others is the grace God wants him to show the assaulter.

Sam says, "I know my story is not over, and though my heart is heavy, I must trust my heavenly Father to reach down into Owen's pain and confusion, to destroy the lies he has believed and accepted about his sexual identity, and to become the man God designed him to be."

God responds to us with compassion. He calls us to extend that compassion to those who've hurt our LGBTQ+ loved one and to count on God's compassion to draw our loved one back into His loving embrace.

Today's Choice: Read Psalm 103:8–14. How do you feel when you read that God does not "harbor his anger forever" and "does not treat us as our sins deserve"? Ask God to remove any desire for vengeance from your heart and replace it with compassion for those who have hurt you or your loved one.

Reflections:

_____

_____

_____

_____

_____

Were You a Long Way Off?

So he set out and came to his father. But while he was still a long way off, his father saw him and felt compassion for him, and ran and embraced him and kissed him.

—LUKE 15:20 (NASB)

Often the loved one struggling with or living under the label of LGBTQ+ is the person we focus on. But if we concentrate on our loved one's relationship with the Lord instead of our own, our vision becomes blurred and short-sighted.

Of course you desire that your loved one returns to the Lord or finds Him for the first time. But focusing on your loved one and his or her faith journey can hinder your ability to either remember how far away from God you are now or once were. At one point in your faith journey, you were the son who "set off for a distant country and there squandered his wealth" (Luke 15:13). The good news is, God brought you home, didn't He?

Your faith journey is exactly that—*your* journey. Instead of indulging in a pity party or spiraling downward into bitterness, ask yourself, "What is God teaching me during this part of my journey?" He is not working against you at this time; He is working for you and in you.

He knows the strength, wisdom, comfort, and faith-building tools each of us need. He has already mapped out our journey and our destination. Let go of the fears or selfish motivations that may keep you from moving forward. What may look like the shorter route to where we want to be may actually take us farther away from Him, and we, like the son in the parable, may wind up in a pigsty of misery.

As you start a new day, remember the story Jesus told of the younger son in Luke 15. "He came to his senses" and went home (Luke 15:17). When he recognized his foolishness, he returned home determined to ask for forgiveness and mercy. The father, who had been watching and waiting, received his son with open arms of compassion. He then told his servants to prepare an enormous feast in celebration of his son's return.

Reflect on the joy God felt when you returned home to Him. God will feel that same joy when your loved one returns. Today He is waiting and watching for that return. Are you waiting and watching in confident expectation too?

Today's Choice: Read Luke 15:11–32. Put yourself in the place of each character—younger son, father, and older son. What can you learn about your situation by identifying with each of them?

Reflections:

_____

_____

_____

_____

_____

Healer of Your Soul

"Fear not; for I am with you; be not dismayed; for I am your God: I will strengthen you; yes, I will help you; I will uphold you with My righteous right hand."

—Isaiah 41:10 (NKJV)

After passing through what seemed a long period of darkness, despair, and weakness, I came to a point of emptiness—a cathartic emptiness of will, power, and strength.

This emptying of self brought me to my knees—on the floor, actually—seeking God like never before. I wept, yelled, and argued until I sensed the emptiness, which was followed by a profound silence. I felt so alone, longing to hear God's voice.

Deep within my soul, I recognized the silence was His way of encouraging me to search my heart, feelings, and thoughts. He wanted me to identify the disobedience of not living out the faith I believed in. This was an opportunity for intense self-examination—deep cleansing of heart, mind, and spirit.

I thought of Job who suffered so much loss, of Joseph whose family plotted against him, of Moses who was driven away from his family into exile, and of David who was betrayed by his friends and his son. God had a plan for those individuals, and I needed to accept that He has a plan for my circumstances—just as He has a plan for yours.

When God takes us into this profound silence, He promises to meet us there—to strengthen us, to help us, and to uphold us with His right hand of righteousness. In that place of helplessness, I released my will and my plans. And when I was emptied, I was ready to embrace His plan. I no longer had the energy to hold His will at a distance or attempt to twist it to fit my wants and needs.

Have you come to that place of surrender? Your soul craves satisfaction; it longs for an end to emotional and spiritual distress. Release control, and your soul will find satisfaction in God.

The healing comes through the silence. When we are still, God reaches down to lift us up. When we are still, He can remove the burden from our back and place it on His shoulders.

As you obey and seek God in the silence, you begin to receive the healing you felt was impossible. The darkness and pain dissipate as your loving heavenly Father massages your heart, your mind, and your soul. You've submitted to the Healer's gentle hands. His presence and His loving touch bring the comfort and strength you need to rise and walk forward.

Today's Choice: Read Isaiah 41:1–13. What does God declare about Himself and then promise to Israel in this passage? Do you believe that these promises apply to you too? Why?

Reflections:

_____

_____

_____

_____

_____

Bringing Back Joy

You will show me the path of life; in Your presence is fullness of joy;
at your right hand are pleasures forevermore.

—Psalm 16:11 (NKJV)

Nicole wondered if she would ever feel joy again. She felt like her heart weighed fifty pounds, and the pressure in her chest made it difficult to breathe.

She attempted to view her circumstances as temporal and conquerable, but as each day ended, the same message replayed in her head: No hope, no relief in sight. She'd read dozens of articles and books on how to bring joy back. She'd tried meditation, positive thinking, charity work, and exercise. Nothing worked. As a Christian, she knew she could cry out to God for help, but she resisted.

Lying in bed one night, she reached rock bottom. In desperation, she knelt on the floor beside her bed and finally released all her thoughts and feelings to God. She poured out her disappointment with herself, her circumstances, and with Him.

Then she heard His voice speak deep within her heart: "Come to me, Nicole. Give Me your burden and joyless days. Allow Me to heal your heart so you feel joy once again." Never had she heard His voice so clearly or felt His presence so intensely.

God is the source of joy, and only as we remain in close relationship with Him can we access joy. Joy doesn't mean that we pretend to be happy during sad circumstances; it is an outpouring of the Holy Spirit—only He can enable us to respond to life's difficult circumstances with that inner contentment and satisfaction.

Trust is difficult during times of suffering. But the apostle James shows us the relationship between trust and joy: "My brethren, count it all joy when you fall into various trials, knowing that the testing of your faith produces patience" (James 1:3 NKJV). Ouch. Those words seem cruel unless our heart is ready to receive them.

Ultimately, we can respond to life's trials with genuine joy if we trust that the Lord has a purpose for allowing those difficult times. James 1:3 suggests that one purpose for trials is to produce patience—the ability to endure, hold up under a trial.

Knowing our loving heavenly Father is doing something specific in our lives, something that will ultimately bring about good, helps us respond with genuine joy. Life's trials are certainly not fun, but we can react to those painful situations with joy if we recognize that God is demonstrating His tough love for us through those circumstances.

The Holy Spirit restored Nicole's joy as she placed her trust in Him. Will you allow Him to restore yours?

Today's Choice: Read Psalm 16. What steps does David take to restore his joy? What step toward joy will you take today?

Reflections:

_____

_____

_____

_____

_____

Overcoming the Darkness

And God said, "Let there be light," and there was light.
God saw that the light was good, and he separated the light from the darkness.

—Genesis 1:3–4

When I withdrew from life because of my dad's desire to be a woman, darkness seemed overpowering. I felt like I was fighting against an invincible opponent. Weighed down with sadness, I had no energy. I wanted to raise my white flag of surrender. The light of Jesus Christ seemed so far off.

Some may ask, "Why didn't you pray?" Let's be honest. I was so beaten down by a spirit intent on my destruction that prayer didn't seem strong enough when my dad left to become Becky or years later when I read his letters to other men, which revealed his confused mind and tortured soul.

Confessing that we need healing to emerge from the darkness is the first step. We long for the life we had before our loved one identified as LGBTQ+. Even more than the wisdom of Jesus' teachings, one of the first things that comes to mind when we think of His ministry was His supernatural power of healing.

Whether it's the darkness overpowering our heart, a cycle of sinful behavior, or another struggle, the light of Jesus' love will always be strong enough to overpower any darkness we face—and save us forever!

Jesus is God incarnate, and God is the giver of life. The world was a dark and formless void until God's first creative act: "Let there be light" (Genesis 1:3). According to John 1:4 the light of Jesus also brought life-giving power: "In him was life, and the life was the light of men" (ESV).

Sometimes we feel lost in the darkness even though we've accepted God's gift of salvation. We may know Jesus is the light, but we find it difficult to navigate our trial without a physical presence to guide us. Yet His life-giving power within us can still light our way when we cannot see or feel His presence.

People often say life gets worse before it gets better. That's not what we want to hear when we're sitting in darkness. But when I've crawled toward Jesus in my weakness, He has always given me the strength and guidance to find Him. Following Jesus will always direct our path toward the true source of light in the darkness. Following Jesus will also carry us into the much brighter horizon of a new tomorrow.

Crawl toward Him today. Let Him bring you into the light of His comfort, strength, and hope.

Today's Choice: Read Genesis 1:1–5 and John 1:1–9. Ask God to separate the light from the darkness in your current circumstances and direct your path today.

Reflections:

_____

_____

_____

_____

_____

Defeat or Victory?

Give thanks in all circumstances;
for this is the will of God in Christ Jesus for you.

—1 THESSALONIANS 5:18 (ESV)

As you walk the journey of a loved one identifying as LGBTQ+, other people may seem to enjoy a better life than yours. But comparing yourself to others is unwise and unrealistic. You probably don't know what burdens other families bear or the losses they've suffered. Maybe a loved one is addicted to drugs, alcohol, or pornography. They may be reeling from a martial affair or caring for a parent with Alzheimer's. A child may have a chronic illness or be a runaway.

If we fall into Satan's trap that our lives aren't unfolding according to plan, self-pity knocks on our heart and wants to take up permanent residence in our mind. In its company, we sulk and obsess over our hurts—real or perceived—and ask God a thousand times, "Why me?" The louder we cry out, the less likely we are to hear His whispered response: "Why not you?"

Every human being leans toward self-pity at some point. Our sin nature is self-centered, and we are hardwired to protect our rights and pursue what we think we deserve. After all, don't we have a say in how our own life should unfold? That mindset is the core of our rebellion against God—we think we should be in charge of the universe, and when we're unable to control events and people, we may grow angry and bitter.

When self is dominant, God is shoved aside. In a sense, we've become our own god. C. S. Lewis said, "The moment you have a self at all, there is a possibility of putting yourself first—wanting to be the center—wanting to be God, in fact. That was the sin of Satan: and that was the sin he taught the human race."[1] Satan wanted to be God Himself, and that caused his fall

---

1 C. S. Lewis, *Mere Christianity* Book II, chapter 3 (NY: Macmillan, 1952), 53.

from heaven (Isaiah 14:12–14). His rebellion was fueled by what he thought he deserved.

Don't allow the what-ifs and could-haves replay endlessly in your head. Instead, let go and obey the One who entrusted you with this difficult, painful journey. Every time you veer toward self-pity, count your blessings instead, especially the redemption Jesus provided on the cross.

When we choose to focus on the Lord Jesus Christ instead of our problems, we have stepped toward the victory He has ordained for our loved ones and for us—in this life and the next. Will you choose defeat or victory?

Today's Choice: Read 1 Thessalonians 5:16–24. What prescription for avoiding self-pity is given in this passage? Are you ready to cling to the promise of verse 24? Why?

Reflections:

_____

_____

_____

_____

_____

God Will Cover You

He will cover you with his feathers, and under his wings you will find refuge;
his faithfulness will be your shield and rampart.

—Psalm 91:4

When Frank learned his daughter was transitioning, he felt so weak and broken. How would he ever get back on his feet? He considered himself a failure as a father and a husband. Why couldn't he have protected his child from this destructive behavior or his wife, Louise, from this pain?

But Frank continued to seek God, asking for strength and His covering. Each morning, he read his Bible as he drank his coffee. The psalmist's metaphor of a mother bird shielding her baby with her wings comforted him.

God feeds, nurtures, and protects His children as they go through trials. Nothing can pull us from the shelter of God's wings; however, we can choose to leave His protection. If we seek God's refuge in our circumstances, He'll provide safety and comfort. The shelter of His wings is the safest place to be.

Hundreds of years after Psalm 91:4 was written, God sent His Son, Jesus, to provide salvation through faith in Him. God wants us to hold on to His faithfulness, which is our "shield and rampart"—that is, our spiritual protection. The shield is held close to the body to protect the heart; the rampart is the surrounding wall of a fortress, which provides freedom to walk about in safety. God provides layers of protection for His children.

We show our faithfulness, our confidence in God by believing He will fulfill His promises. We can count on Him being there for us. When we call out to Him, He will help. Our emotions are a gift from God, and He gives us the freedom to express them openly in His presence. We can pour out our grief, fear, and uncertainty.

Each day Frank reminds himself that God is a refuge for him and Louise, no matter what they face. They cling to the hope that God's faithful care and continual presence will bring them through this challenging journey.

God is our refuge in trouble. In Him we find safety, calmness, and hope. Our faith in God does not exempt us from difficulties, but God will protect us and sustain us, no matter how dark or difficult the path ahead.

Are you feeling overwhelmed today—weakened and broken by your circumstances? Call out to the God who loves you and nestle under the protection of His wings. He will bring strength and healing.

Today's Choice: Read Psalm 91. Note God's "I will" statements in verses 14–16. Do you believe that God will fulfill those promises for you and your loved ones? Why?

Reflections:

_____

_____

_____

_____

_____

Restoration Is Coming

Then the Lord said to Satan, "Have you considered my servant Job? There is no one on earth like him; he is blameless and upright, a man who fears God and shuns evil."

—JOB 1:8

When Loretta's son transitioned to take on a female persona, she felt numb. Every time she and her husband, Jake, began to process their son's status, he moved deeper into his false identity, and his parents fell apart again.

"I feel like Job," Loretta said, "scraping my leg with a pottery shard, oblivious to the comfort or advice others offer. I feel as abandoned by God as he did."

Perhaps you know that feeling.

Satan wants to use our troubles to draw us away from God; however, God wants to use those situations to draw us closer to Him. God allowed Satan to bring trouble into Job's life. In a single day, Job received news that his oxen, donkeys, and camels were stolen; many of his servants were killed; his sheep and shepherds were burned up in a fire; and his ten children were killed in a storm (Job 1:1–19).

Job and several of his friends engaged in many discussions about why the bad things happened; then God Himself spoke to Job and gave him a glimpse of His immense wisdom and character. When Job realized his life was a tiny part of something grander than he had ever imagined, he stopped questioning God's trustworthiness.

Loretta was in that frustrating, dark place of questioning God, but our gracious God wouldn't allow her to stay there—just as He didn't allow Job to stay in his dark place.

God can work through the pain inflicted by others' choices and fulfill His purpose in your life, in your loved one's life, and in the world. Will you allow God into your pain and bewildering situation, or will you let Satan drive you away from God and into despair?

In the midst of your suffering, you can respond as Job did: "The Lord gave and the Lord has taken away; may the name of the Lord be praised" (Job 1:21). Scripture then adds that "in all this, Job did not sin by charging God with wrongdoing" (v. 22).

Whatever your troubles, know that God hasn't forsaken you. The One who allows these dark days won't waste your suffering. God can work through your suffering to accomplish greater good than you can imagine. He'll never stop working to build you up, to restore your hope, and to bring healing.

And one day, like Job and Loretta, you'll say, "May the name of the Lord be praised."

Today's Choice: Read Job 1 and Job 42. How did God restore what He had allowed Satan to take from Job? How is He restoring what you have lost?

Reflections:

_____

_____

_____

_____

_____

Courageous Transparency

Carry each other's burdens, and in this way you will fulfill the law of Christ.

—GALATIANS 6:2

The Sunday morning worship service began like any other. After a few worship songs, Pastor Steven walked to the podium. But his prayer signaled that something unordinary was about to happen: "Thank You, God, for who You are. Thank You for giving me courage today to share my heart about something difficult and heartbreaking. Bless the ears that hear and open their hearts not only to us, but others as well."

Pastor Steven then spoke on biblical sexuality and gender. At the end of the sermon, he motioned for his wife, Anne, to join him onstage.

"Anne and I want to run and hide from you and God, but that isn't the answer. We're hurting, but we want to be transparent with you. Those who know our daughter Scarlett or have friended her on social media may know what I'm talking about. Instead of rumors and untruths being spread, Anne and I want to state publicly that Scarlett has come out as a lesbian. We're just beginning this journey, but we've learned one thing: not talking about these issues in church hasn't benefited us.

"As your pastor, forgive me for ignoring such a prevalent issue in our society. Anne and I don't have the answers, but we're trusting God to guide us. We love Scarlett and that will never change. When Scarlett comes back to God—and I say when because I trust God to bring her back to Him—please see her as a God does. She's a lost young woman, trying to discover who she is but searching in the wrong places. If you see her, please greet her in love as God would. Don't judge her; pray for her. And pray for us as we pray for you.

"Don't be afraid to speak about LGBTQ+ issues at home. Help your children navigate who they are and how to treat peers identifying as gay or transgender. God's people have hidden our heads in the sand far too long. We must provide a safe environment for our children to share their struggle or a friend's struggle. If we don't, our silence will push them toward the alternative—the LGBTQ+ community."

You've probably heard the adage, "the church is the only army that shoots its wounded." You may be wrestling with a situation similar to Steven and Anne's. Don't hide your pain. Be courageously transparent before a trusted loved one or mentor. Allow others to help you carry your burden.

> **Today's Choice:** One way to carry each other's burden is intercessory prayer. In fact, the most powerful weapon on earth is prayer—access to the throne room of God (Hebrews 4:14–16).

Use the following prayer as a model:

Dear heavenly Father, Give me the courage to speak about Your true plan for man and woman and godly sexuality in my home, in my church, and in my circle of influence. Give me the loving, age-appropriate words to share with my children or grandchildren. Lastly, show me how to help my church become a safe place for the gay or transgender person looking for You with a sincere heart. Guide us, gracious Father. In Jesus' name, amen.

Reflections:

_____

_____

_____

_____

_____

Moving Forward

Only be strong and very courageous; be careful to do according to all the law which Moses My servant commanded you; do not turn from it to the right or to the left, so that you may have success wherever you go.

—Joshua 1:7 (NASB)

Have you ever wondered why God allows a particular set of circumstances to wreak havoc in your life? Most of us feel like our pain is undeserved, and I doubt any of us would volunteer to walk the journey of a loved one struggling with sexuality, gender, or both.

One of the first truths God wants us to embrace is that broken relationships are not a punishment. He is a merciful God who reaches out to us in love when we suffer, always eager to bring healing. So like every other circumstance, broken relationships are an opportunity to draw close to God, learn from Him, and then move forward.

A broken heart can mess up our thoughts, emotions, and actions. We find it difficult to think straight and make wise decisions. We feel confused and desperate. Because of our emotional attachment to a loved one or a relationship, we may refuse to seek God's advice, thinking He might counsel us to take actions we don't want to take.

So we turn to other people instead—a pastor, a counselor, a friend, or a relative. At first, we may feel better talking to this person or that person, and their advice may be logical and wise. But in the end, their counsel and companionship only soothe our pain for a brief time. Then we begin to look somewhere else for complete satisfaction and peace.

To move forward, we must accept that other people are not God. They do not have the infallible wisdom He wishes to reveal to us through His Word. As God told Joshua before he moved forward with the Israelites into the Promised Land, to have success wherever we go, we need to meditate on God's Word "day and night" and "be careful to do everything written in it" (Joshua 1:8). As we immerse ourselves in His Word, the Holy Spirit will reveal to us the steps we need to take to move forward, and then He'll walk alongside us, giving us the wisdom and strength we need each day. That's what God did for Joshua, and that's what He's willing to do for us too.

Only God can provide what you need to move forward. As you read His Word and obey it, He will surround you and your situation completely. Trust Him to lead you forward. He will do for you what you cannot do yourself.

> **Today's Choice:** Read Joshua 1:1–9. What did Joshua have to leave behind? What promises did God give him to help him move forward? What is God asking you to leave behind in order to move forward?

You may want to use this prayer: Lord, break any barrier that's hindering my advancement and let me experience a great advancement. Lord, I want to move forward in You. In Your name I pray, amen.

Reflections:

_____

_____

_____

_____

_____

Relinquishing Control

Your arm is endowed with power; your hand is strong, your right hand exalted.

—Psalm 89:13

When your loved one(s) shared the news of their sexuality or gender plans, what went through your mind? Like many family members, you may have thought, *What can I do or say to change their mind?* In essence, you wanted to control the situation so you could bring about what you needed or desired.

I said to myself, "If I do this, surely Dad will stay or get help. If I call a counselor or pastor, surely he'll listen to them. If I'm nicer to Dad, his heart will change." I acted out of fear and pretended I had some sort of control.

This tug-of-war is exhausting. You tug one direction until the rope burns become unbearable; at the same time, your loved one pulls the other end with equal determination. Who will win? No one. You both will walk away with bleeding hands and a broken heart because neither of you can control the other.

Another tug-of-war also occurs between you and God. I often told God I was handing the situation over to Him, but I kept grabbing it back—trying one more possible solution on my own. Eventually, though, I ran out of what-ifs, maybe-I-shoulds, and if-onlys. I lived so long under the "no one else" mentality: if something is going to be done, I must do it. I wanted to fix my dad—as if I could be his savior. Admitting that I could not fix him was the first step toward relinquishing control to God. I had to place my trust in God alone—only He could bring healing to me and to my dad.

Get alone with God and consider what makes it so difficult to hand your heartbreak and disappointments to Him. Ask Him to reveal the reasons you struggle to hold on to the rope—burns and all. If you're like me, my refusal to release the rope had two causes: I wanted to fix my problems myself, and I wanted my loved one to seek completeness and obedience in God. How ironic! I wanted my loved one to depend on God even as I insisted on independence from God.

The phrase "let go and let God" is more than a bumper-sticker slogan. It's the only way to navigate the journey of a loved one identifying as LGBTQ+. Relinquishing control is a daily, moment-by-moment choice. But the more consistently you practice this discipline, the more strength God will give you to take the next step.

> **Today's Choice:** Read Psalm 89:9–18. What illustrations of God's strength does the psalmist give? What other attributes of God does he mention? Who receives God's blessing according to verses 15–17?

Reflections:

_____

_____

_____

_____

_____

Come Out of Hiding

He [Adam] answered,
"I heard you in the garden, and I was afraid because I was naked; so I hid."

—GENESIS 3:10

When our small town heard that my dad left our family because he wanted to live as a woman, I wanted to hide in our house. I didn't want to see anyone I knew in the local grocery store or gas station. When someone looked at me, I wondered, *Do they know?* I felt like an outcast, as if I lived in exile.

I was ashamed of my father's decision and didn't know what to say when someone asked, "How's your dad?" Neither did I know how to express my feelings about him or the trauma he'd caused in our family. Some days I cried for no reason; other days no tears would come.

I had done nothing wrong, but the shame of my dad's lifestyle felt like a thousand-pound elephant sitting on my chest. How could I possibly lift it? I allowed other people's reactions and words lodge deep in my soul, and the shame grew heavier and heavier.

But finally I realized that shame was not a weight God wanted me to carry. I needed to let go of the idea that I was in some way responsible for Dad's choices. I could not have prevented his decision to live his life as he chose. I had no way to stop him, even though I attempted to change his mind and behavior again and again.

Although some may think God was absent in my circumstances or that He expected me to just move on and get over my dad's choices (like many suggest), God was always present.

In the garden of Eden, God searched for Adam and Eve after they sinned because He wanted to remove the shame they felt. They, of course, felt shame because of their own wrongdoing, but we can also feel shame because of what our loved ones do. Either way, God comes looking for us and says, "Where are you? Stop hiding and let Me help you."

God won't allow us to run away from our circumstances no matter how badly we wish to; instead, He asks us to turn our circumstances over to Him. Just as He clothed Adam and Eve with animal skins, He clothes us with Jesus' pure robes of righteousness. We are covered, we are clean, and we can hold our head high.

Come out of hiding. Let God comfort you and clothe you. Let Him lead you forward.

Today's Choice: Compare Genesis 3:21 with 1 Corinthians 1:30 and Revelation 19:7–8. Can you see yourself as clothed in "fine linen, bright and clean"? Why?

Reflections:

_____

_____

_____

_____

_____

The Message of the Cross

Let this mind be in you which was also in Christ Jesus . . . being found in appearance as a man, He humbled Himself and became obedient to the point of death, even the death of the cross.

—Philippians 2:5, 8 (NKJV)

When we're in physical pain, we seek out physicians or holistic methods to restore our health. If we need emotional or mental help, we may turn to counselors, pastors, or life coaches. We usually pray about these matters, believing God wants us to be well. But when it comes to homosexuality, does the message of the cross really make a difference?

Years ago, Sherry left her husband and son to live with another woman. Sherry was running from the lies the Enemy, Satan, had fed her for far too long. He told her, "Something's wrong with you." That something sent her down a road of more lies and more running from the message of the cross.

Sherry knew all the Bible verses about her homosexual lifestyle. She'd been raised in a Christian home, and her dad was a well-known preacher and gifted speaker. But the Enemy's lies grabbed her at an opportune time when she was feeling unhappy and unfulfilled.

God pursued her until she finally confessed that she was living in emptiness and craving something more than what she had. She sought out reparative therapy to bring healing to her heart and soul in a holistic way.

Her journey toward healing began when she met with a pastoral counselor. He helped her to recognize the lies she believed and to see herself through the eyes of Jesus Christ. She humbled herself and asked for forgiveness. She recommitted herself to a life of obeying God's Word. Prayer was the main counseling support tool her counselor offered, and it worked. Regular prayer helped Sherry understand how the message of the cross makes a difference.

What is the significance of the cross? Philippians 2:5–8 says that we are to have "the same mindset as Christ Jesus . . . he humbled himself by becoming obedient to death—even death on a cross." Jesus manifested two attitudes at the cross—humility and obedience.

Our healing begins as we allow the Holy Spirit to cultivate these attitudes in us. He'll help us better understand why suffering and loss are necessary. God is setting us free from self: self-sufficiency and self-direction. In our suffering, we experience "the power of his resurrection and participation in his sufferings, becoming like him in his death" (Philippians 3:10).

So yes, the cross is necessary. It brings us to the end of ourselves, and only there can we begin our healing. Are you ready to embrace the message of the cross?

Today's Choice: Read Philippians 2:1–11. In what areas is God asking you to humble yourself and be obedient? What step can you take toward humble obedience today?

Reflections:

_____

_____

_____

_____

_____

Do You Remember Me?

Lord, you are the God who saves me; day and night I cry out to you.

—PSALM 88:1

A loving grandfather shares, "There was a time when I shouted out, 'Lord, do you remember me?'" If we're honest, most of us relate to a point on this specific journey when we questioned if God was really with us. The grandfather confessed, "I cried and cried, asking God to not forget our family and our grandchild who needed Him so very much."

A fog of dread and despair over our circumstances can darken our lives. You feel powerless when confronted with your inability to influence someone else's decisions on how to live or how he or she chooses to deal with denial, pain, and distance from God.

You feel alone. You wonder if you're the only person going through this set of circumstances, yet you are too scared to talk with people around you. When someone asks, "How you are?" you put on your Christian mask and say, "I'm fine, and you?"

Then one day, a ray of hope penetrates your darkness. As you search the internet for help, you discover you are not the only one. Others have faced their situation and reached out—maybe in desperation. You take the risk and make a connection with others who have experienced similar pain.

The many hours of dwelling on the problem have stolen hours of your life. Through sharing with others, you realize the Enemy of your soul created an environment of worry and doubt, where you were imprisoned for a long time.

The key to overcoming despair is focusing your thoughts on the Lord, which will keep you in a peaceful state of mind. God desires to bring restoration to the destruction the Enemy has done. As you continue to trust and stay committed to God, you'll experience more healing. Finding a community of likeminded believers who can identify with your situation and walk alongside you is also crucial to your restoration.

Certain signposts point to the reality that God remembers us. First, He assures us that He hears our prayers for help. Second, He sends help—through His Word, a book, a song, a podcast, a person, or a support group. As we train our spiritual eyes to recognize these signs of remembrance, we'll see more and more of them.

Take your eyes off your circumstances. Focus on God. Allow difficulty to bring you to your knees in prayer. Cry for help, then watch for deliverance. Help is on the way.

Today's Choice: Read Psalm 88. What is the writer's state of mind in this psalm? How does verse 1 convey a ray of hope? What ray of hope has God given you today?

Reflections:

_____

_____

_____

_____

_____

Cling to God's Love

The faithful love of the Lord never ends! His mercies never cease.
Great is his faithfulness; his mercies begin afresh each morning.

—LAMENTATIONS 3:22–23 (NLT)

Does God really love me? Painful circumstances often prompt us to ask that question. After all, if He loves us, how could He bring so much pain into our life?

"Jesus loves me this I know, for the Bible tells me so" works fine as long as life sails along. But when a loved one embraces the LGBTQ+ lifestyle, we family members feel alone, isolated, bitter, and unloved.

When Daisy received the unimaginable news of her daughter's sexual sins, she screamed at God, "Take the very air in my lungs and give me death. I can't hear any more." She felt like her heart had shattered into a million pieces—impossible to mend. Maybe you find yourself in Daisy's place—angry at God and longing for death, surrounded by the darkness of your circumstances and wracked with pain.

Trying to reconcile God's love and mercy with our suffering is scary and often leads us to question His character. After all, He could have put a roadblock in your loved one's life and redirected them to a different road, right?

Satan loves to put us in that mindset. He likes to tell us that submitting to God as we question His love isn't a big problem. But eventually, that whispered questioning of God's love will lead us into direct rebellion against Him. We can't rest in the knowledge that God is in complete control while we doubt His love and goodness.

The prophet Jeremiah was overcome with grief when the Babylonians destroyed Jerusalem. He wrote, "[God] has besieged me and surrounded me with bitterness and hardship. He has made me dwell in darkness like those long dead. . . . Even when I call out or cry for help, he shuts out my prayer" (Lamentations 3:5–8).

You may feel that way about your situation too. Satan may be whispering, "Surely if God loved you, this wouldn't be happening to you." Don't listen to his lie. God's love is real—unconditional and unending. Jeremiah also wrote, "Though [God] brings grief, he will show compassion, so great is his unfailing love" (Lamentations 3:32).

God's love for you cost Him His only Son, Jesus Christ. No matter how besieged, broken, bitter, or isolated you feel, don't give up on God's love for you or your loved one. God's love has no limits and no end. Let Him love you.

Today's Choice: Read Lamentations 3:1–26. How did Jeremiah move past his anguish and into hope? What step forward toward hope can you take today?

Reflections:

_____

_____

_____

_____

_____

Is God Your Crutch?

O my people, listen to my instructions. Open your ears to what I am saying.

—Psalm 78:1 (NLT)

God sometimes seems so far away when we're in pain, and His words seem as unreachable as the stars. But, in truth, He is right beside us.

In Psalm 78, the writer speaks with authority as he implores his people to pay attention to what God has done in the past. He reminds his listeners that even though their ancestors refused to live by God's law, God still did miracles in their sight (Psalm 78:10–12). You may wonder how God's people could be so ungrateful. How could they be so ignorant and insensible to God's transcendent goodness and patient instruction?

We could ask the same question about ourselves.

For a time, God allows us to wallow in sorrow, guilt, and uncertainty. Our heart is broken, and the pain seems unbearable. In these times, though, God offers support to help us manage life, just as a physician offers a set of crutches to an injured person.

The Holy Spirit is our support. Crutches are strong enough to bear someone's weight and can be adjusted to their height; likewise, the Holy Spirit is strong enough to bear the heavy weight of your suffering and adjusts His support to meet your needs.

We must choose to receive His help, though. During a difficult time of my life, I lay flat on the floor, feeling lifeless. I had no strength left to fight back or change the situation. I called out to God, "What have I done so wrong to be afflicted time and time again?"

I needed the support only God could give me. Would I allow God to be my crutch, holding me up when I could no longer stand? Or would I refuse His help out of pride, anger, resentment, or pain?

Perhaps you've reached that desperate stage today. Peace of mind and strength to move forward are within reach if you let God be your support. He loves you deeply and longs to begin a new healing in you.

Throughout the most difficult times, my relationship with God has been more important than any connection to another person. He has been my crutch and held me steady when I had no strength. I depend on Him to get me through life's valleys and mountains. He is my crutch, and I'm so grateful for His constant support.

Don't be too proud to call out for help or too stubborn to lean on The Crutch.

Today's Choice: Read Psalm 78. How does God prove His faithfulness again and again in spite of His people's faithlessness? In what ways do these examples prove His willingness to be The Crutch for you?

Reflections:

_____

_____

_____

_____

_____

Resting in the Wisdom of God

And I, when I came to you, brothers, did not come proclaiming to you the testimony of God with lofty speech or wisdom. For I decided to know nothing among you except Jesus Christ and him crucified. And I was with you in weakness and in fear and much trembling, and my speech and my message were not in plausible words of wisdom, but in demonstration of the Spirit and of power, that your faith might not rest in the wisdom of men but in the power of God.

—1 Corinthians 2:1–5 (ESV)

When bad news comes your way, where do you turn? You may first turn inward, seeking to hide from the news itself and from others who may know about your circumstances. Later, however, comes the urge to connect with someone, to share the weight of your burden. You may hope this other person can give you advice or affirm the decisions you're making.

Maria attempted to ease her burden that way. The first person offered direction from God's Word, but Maria didn't like the answers. She wanted an easier way to extend love to her daughter who had come out as transgender. One friend suggested, "Being transgender really isn't that big of a deal. Just love her." This viewpoint was supported by two others who said, "It's only a phase" and "It's only a name change and clothing differences." The more people Maria approached, the more obsessed she became with finding what she considered the best answer for her. But each new answer brought more confusion.

Paul reminded his fellow believers in Corinth that he didn't use "plausible words of wisdom" when he proclaimed the "testimony of God." He didn't attempt to sound wise by formulating persuasive arguments or substituting his wisdom for God's. He desired only that his listeners know "Jesus Christ and him crucified"—what Jesus accomplished by sacrificing his life so every person could be forgiven and reconciled to God. God alone was the source of the wisdom Paul made known, and the wisdom he offered was centered on Christ and what God accomplished through him.

Asking a friend or loved one to come alongside us as we seek God's will is beneficial. We need others to pray with us and for us. But if seeking the counsel of others replaces our desire to seek God, we may miss out on a "demonstration of the Spirit and of power that [our] faith might not rest in the wisdom of men but in the power of God."

You and I could ask a million people what they would do in our situation. We can keep asking until someone gives us an answer that feels good (for a short period). But like Maria, we'll just end up more confused, more uncertain in the long run.

Continue to rest in God. Seek His wisdom and guidance first, then test the value of all other advice you receive by what God clearly reveals to you.

Today's Choice: Read 1 Corinthians 2:1–16. What is the Holy Spirit's role in imparting the wisdom of God to us? Do you believe He will also direct you in your current situation? Why?

Reflections:

_____

_____

_____

_____

_____

Can't Make a Decision?

"For I know the plans I have for you," declares the Lord,
"plans to prosper you and not to harm you, plans to give you hope and a future."

—JEREMIAH 29:11

When Nichelle's daughter Sarah came out as a lesbian, Nichelle called her sister, Julie. She knew she could trust Julie with her pain and anguish. Sarah wanted her mom to accept her relationship with her partner, Anne. But Julie didn't support Nichelle's decision about Anne, so Nichelle called someone else for advice.

Sometimes people go from one person to another or one ministry to another seeking the answer they want. Like Nichelle, you may go back and forth over the options, overanalyze, and ask others for their opinions before you finally act. But if an answer from another person goes against God's design, will, or Word, you won't feel any satisfaction in your spirit.

As we grow spiritually, we learn a much better way to make decisions. One intuitive approach to decision-making is always available to us: prayer and patience. All we have to do is implement it.

Will you give God the time needed to discover His guidance? Relying solely on human advice can have devastating results, but seeking God's will and waiting patiently for Him to reveal the next step can lead to restoration and healing.

As you seek answers from God, first frame your attitude into one of trust and obedience. There's no reason to be fearful about decisions when you're secure in the knowledge that God has your best interest in mind. Before you were ever born, He established "plans to give you a hope and a future." He also ordained good plans for your LGBTQ+ loved one.

First, ask God if the decision involves a moral area or non-moral area. Discerning the will of God in moral areas is usually easier because God's Word often provides clear direction. If God has already revealed His will about a situation in Scripture, you have one decision to make: listen and obey or deny what His Word says. Submission to God's written Word is essential. When your will is humbly and fully submitted to the Master, you can be confident He'll illuminate your path.

Seeking God for answers takes both time and a deep desire to hear His voice. Don't look to other people for a quick fix. Be prepared to resubmit your will over and over again to God throughout the process. Scripture tells us that confident faith pleases God (Hebrews 11:6), so seek Him diligently with confidence that He'll reveal His will and then wait for His response.

Today's Choice: Read Jeremiah 29:1–14. What did God want His people to do while they waited for His good plan (return to Jerusalem) to come to pass? What might He want you to do as you wait for Him to bring restoration to you and your family?

Reflections:

_____

_____

_____

_____

_____

His Light Will Dawn

Even in darkness light dawns for the upright,
for those who are gracious and compassionate and righteous.

—PSALM 112:4

Barbara begged God many times to rescue her son, James, from his LGBTQ+ lifestyle. He was brokenhearted because his parents refused to bless his same-sex relationships. "You treat my partner with respect and kindness when you see him," he said, "but I know you don't approve of our relationship. And refusing to give your full support is cruel." Consequently, James distanced himself from them more and more.

His attitude grieved Barbara and her husband, Eddy. They desperately wanted to restore the close relationship they'd had with James before he chose a same-sex partner. Their inability to bless the relationship seemed to imprison them in a dark hole. For so long, Barbara felt like she trudged through each day weighed down by heavy chains fastened to her wrists, ankles, and chest.

But one day when she awoke, slipped out of bed, and stretched her arms, she felt lighter. Looking up at the ceiling, she called out, "God, You've done something. I feel it in my heart, spirit, and body." She walked over to the bedroom window and said, "Praise Your mighty name, Jesus Christ. You've taken the darkness and weight from me."

Tears wet Barbara's cheeks as she continued to praise God. For the first time in several years, she felt God's joy, mercy, and love in a powerful way. God's light had finally driven away the darkness. She couldn't wait to tell Eddy when he returned home from work.

She was gardening that afternoon when Eddy arrived. She stood quickly and walked toward him. "Wait till you hear what God did for me today." They walked back into the house and sat at the kitchen table. She reached for his hand and told her story.

When she finished, Eddy said, "I've been asking God to encourage us, to show us He's with us. Your experience this morning is God's answer to my prayers." He shook his head. "Sometimes we wonder if God's listening when we pray and pray and pray about a situation." Eddy squeezed her hand and smiled. "He does, Barbara, He does!"

Eddy closed his eyes and prayed, "Loving Father, my heart is bursting with joy for the gift You gave Barbara and me today. We continue to trust You with James and ask You to bring him back home to You first, then to us. In Jesus' name, amen."

The light will dawn on you, too, as you continue to call out to God for help. He'll answer your prayers, and you'll feel His joy, mercy, and love again as powerfully as Barbara and Eddy did.

Today's Choice: Read Psalm 112:1–4. In what ways are the blessings of verses 2–4 related to the conditions of verse 1? In what ways are you honoring God and delighting in His commands?

Reflections:

_____

_____

_____

_____

_____

Time to Choose

See, God has come to save me. I will trust in him and not be afraid.
The Lord God is my strength and my song; he has given me victory.

—Isaiah 12:2 (NLT)

When Virginia's daughter, Emily, left a letter announcing she was a lesbian, Virginia and her husband, Adam, were distraught. Several years earlier, their son had also come out as gay, then transgender. Both Virginia and Adam recognized the root issues that can create the stirring in one's heart for a same-sex relationship. But that didn't make their daughter's decision any easier to bear.

Six months later, Adam had a fatal heart attack. For Virginia, the loss of her spouse was compounded by the absence of someone who understood the pain of her daughter's lesbian lifestyle. She was confident, though, that God was with her, and she clung to the promise that God would be her strength.

She then received another letter from Emily, announcing that she and her partner, Adela, were getting married. "God, where are You?" Virginia prayed. "I've always done what You've asked. I cared for my mom without complaint as her health deteriorated. When Emily came out as gay, I felt betrayed, but I did not complain. You took my dear husband away from me, yet I did not complain. But I ask You, Lord, why this? Not only is Emily marrying another woman, but Adele is bringing her three children into this marriage. How much more heartache do You think I can take?"

Knowing she needed some time alone with God, Virginia drove to a favorite mountain hiking trail. At the end of her trek, she sat on a rock and viewed the vista below her.

I have a choice, she thought. *I can follow the advice Job's wife gave him and "Curse God and die!" (Job 2:9). I can give up and reject God who seems to have abandoned me. Or I can follow the prophet Isaiah's example and depend on God to give me victory over fear and heal my pain.*

"Lord," Virginia prayed, "I choose You. I choose to believe that You will help me be a godly influence in my children's lives and in the lives of Adele and her children. Please show me the next step. In Your name I pray, amen."

God never asks us to figure it all out on our own. He asks us to trust Him, to recognize His leadership and sovereignty in our lives, and to believe that He will provide victory over whatever is troubling us. God will direct our steps through His Word. Don't try to walk this road alone. Choose to move forward with God.

Today's Choice: Read Job 1:9–10 and Isaiah 12:2–6. Which attitude are you leaning toward today—despair or praise? Ask God to show you reasons to praise Him.

Reflections:

_____

_____

_____

_____

_____

Purpose in the Storm

"Teacher, do you not care that we are perishing?"

—MARK 4:38 (NKJV)

Riding out storms is difficult. When the waves crash and torrential rain pelts us, escaping or hiding from the storm seems the best way to handle our circumstances. But just as the disciples endured the hurricane-force storm on the Sea of Galilee for a while, we may also have to wait for Jesus to calm the wind and clear the sky.

You may want to say, "Get me out of this as soon as possible." But if God allows a storm to blow into your life, He has a plan and purpose. He wants your attention. And let's be honest, when someone close to us is living a LGBTQ+ life, God has our attention.

The disciples' faith in Jesus was tested in the storm. They questioned His character, implying that He did not care whether they lived or died. We may feel the same way when we face emotional and spiritual distress. The broken relationships that result from a loved one's pursuit of the LGBTQ+ lifestyle threaten our peace, comfort, and joy. They plunge us into waves of fear, doubt, and hopelessness. Like the disciples, we may cry out, "Don't you care about what's happening to me, my family, my loved ones?"

Someone close to us may bring on the storm; other times our decisions create the storm. The longer you hold on to the thought that it's all about your loved one, the longer it'll take for you to realize this storm is also about you. To survive the storm, you'll need to loosen your grip on the helm and allow God to steer the boat. Asking God to take control may be difficult, but humble surrender demonstrates your obedience and faithfulness.

God doesn't want the storm to destroy us; He wants the storm to strengthen us—make us better sailors. Begin the growth process by admitting your grief and pain, then express your anger and disappointment to God.

Next, allow Him to speak to you through His Word. Claim His promises of rescue and healing, of protection and guidance.

Our storm may last much longer than the one the disciples faced that day on the Sea of Galilee. But Jesus is the captain of our circumstances, and He will navigate us into calmer waters. In the meantime, focus on Him—His faithfulness, His power, His love. Study His Word, and surround yourself with supportive, godly people.

Trust your captain. The storm will end, and the sky will clear.

Today's Choice: Read Mark 4:35–41. Why do you think Jesus was sleeping in the boat? What do His questions in verse 40 indicate about the purpose of the storm? What are you learning about yourself and about Jesus in your storm?

Reflections:

_____

_____

_____

_____

_____

A Safe Place

*Be devoted to one another in brotherly love. Honor one another above
yourselves. . . . Rejoice with those who rejoice; mourn with those who mourn.*

—ROMANS 12: 10, 15

L iam forced a smile as he approached the backyard deck where a group
of men had gathered for the Saturday morning men's Bible study. Why
had he come? The urge to turn, run, and hide was strong, but something
compelled him forward.

As the other men greeted him, Liam poured a cup of coffee but skipped
the donut.

His friend Jacob chuckled. "What's the matter, Liam? You never turn
down a sweet."

Liam leaned on the railing and looked out toward the wooded area
behind the house.

Several other men made eye contact with Jacob, indicating he should
speak first.

Jacob cleared his throat. "Hey buddy, whatever's happening, you can tell
us. Anything you share goes no further than this group."

An uncomfortable silence followed.

Scott, the group's leader, stood and bowed his head. "God, Liam's
struggling with something. Assure him that whatever it is, he can tell us.
We care deeply for him and his family. We are a safe place for him. In Jesus'
name, amen."

Liam approached the picnic table where the other men sat. "When
Samantha came home from college last weekend, she told Sherry and me
that she's a lesbian, that she's moving in with the girl she loves." He sipped
his coffee. "I don't know what to do. Sherry wants to hide from everyone
and pretend this isn't happening. I blame myself. Where did I go wrong as a
father? What could I have done different?"

87

Jacob rose, walked over to Liam, and squeezed his shoulder. "I can't imagine what you and Sherry are going through. But we are here for you."

Levi then stood. "I haven't said anything about what Amanda and I are going through. Too ashamed, really. But our daughter, Lynn, is also living a lesbian life."

The men's group was transformed that morning. The Holy Spirit showed up, filling the men with the courage to provide godly support and encouragement for one another. They committed to accountability—to reveal the truth about the pain they were living with. They promised to walk life out together, to coax one another away from their hiding places into a safe place.

God promises to answer when we call out to Him. Sometimes He answers by providing people who will walk alongside us. If your urge to hide is strong, if feelings of shame seem overwhelming, turn to God. Ask Him to bring someone into your life who will walk this journey with you.

Today's Choice: Read Romans 12:9–15. Friendship and accountability are reciprocal. Who needs your support today? Who can you encourage to "be joyful in hope, patient in affliction, and faithful in prayer"?

Reflections:

_____

_____

_____

_____

_____

Dry Bones Come Back to Life

The hand of the Lord was on me, and he brought me out by the Spirit of the Lord and set me in the middle of a valley; it was full of bones. He led me back and forth among them, and I saw a great many bones on the floor of the valley, bones that were very dry. He asked me, "Son of man, can these bones live?" I said, "Sovereign Lord, you alone know."

—EZEKIEL 37:1–3

C an you recover from the pain you've experiencing? That question demonstrates honesty and uncertainty, just as Ezekiel expressed when he said, "Sovereign Lord, You alone know." Ezekiel seems to be shaking his head and feeling overwhelmed over the enormity of the loss he and the nation of Israel experienced as exiles in Babylon. They lamented, "Our bones are dried up and our hope is gone; we are cut off" (Ezekiel 37:11).

But God doesn't say, "Oh, just snap out of it, Ezekiel." No. God doesn't treat His children that way. Instead, God brings hope and healing to Ezekiel through a vision. God allows him time to process the situation as He leads the prophet back and forth among the dry bones before speaking to him. God may also allow you to ponder the dry bones that surround you—broken relationships and dead dreams. But He will not leave you in that valley alone.

We can choose to focus on what seems out of control when our life seems dead. But chaos and pain are not the final chapter of God's will for you. Just as God told Ezekiel to prophesy to the bones, to tell them that the Lord was going to bring them back to life, you may need to prophesy to yourself—maybe to loved ones too—and speak words of life and healing.

God's Word speaks of abundant life and a prosperous future in many places. In Ezekiel 37, God promises to do something about dry bones ten times:

"I will make breath enter you."

"I will attach tendons to you."

"I will make flesh come upon you."

"I will cover you with skin."

"I am going to open your graves."

"I am going to bring you up from your graves."

"I will put breath in you."

"I will bring you back to your land."

"I will put my Spirit in you."

"I will settle you in your own land."

Three times He says, "And you will live."

In the valley of loss and pain, choose to nurture your soul with these promises. God will breathe life into you again. Refuse to be ruled by uncertainty and doubt. God's love for you and your confidence in Him will generate the courage you need to move beyond your valley of dry bones into the lush fields of abundance.

Today's Choice: Read Ezekiel 37:1–14. In what ways do you feel like "your bones are dried up" today? Which promises in this passage give you hope that you will live again?

Reflections:

_____

_____

_____

_____

_____

Rebuilding a Sense of Normalcy

A time to kill and a time to heal; a time to tear down and a time to build up.

—ECCLESIASTES 3:3 (NLT)

Dealing with his son's gay lifestyle, Robbie battled guilt, loss, and brokenness. He didn't share his pain with anyone. How could others understand if they hadn't faced similar heartache? But the longer he remained silent, the more devastated he felt.

We pass through many difficulties, but a loved one choosing an LGBTQ+ lifestyle seems to impact us spiritually more than many other trials. Your life may have seemed normal, then out of nowhere a family member announces his or her attraction to a same-sex partner or embraces bi-sexuality or—even more dramatic because of the physical changes—a desire to transition to the opposite sex.

When you're blindsided by such news, numbness, bewilderment, and anger are normal. You may even sense an inner deadness—a lack of energy or the will to do normal tasks such as eating, sleeping, or working. Resuming normal life seems impossible.

But you are a child of the all-powerful God! He's the source of all life, and He'll rekindle the desire to live again. Where you are today is not where you will be in the future. No matter how bad your current situation, not only is our God a God of miracles, but He also seeks to open your heart to what's possible as He builds you up and places you on a path to living life again.

In Ecclesiastes 3, Solomon reminds us that "there is a time for everything, and a season for every activity under the heavens" (v. 1). Pay attention to two important words: *everything* and *season*. Every event God allows to enter our life has purpose, and every circumstance He permits is temporary. Rely on His faithfulness and love to lead you through each circumstance and reveal part or all of the purpose in His perfect time.

Rekindling the will to live and rebuilding your life requires nothing other than living in the moment. Walk with Him and give Him access to your heart and soul—even the most tender areas. He is life, so let Him pour that life into you.

Robbie learned to pay close attention to his soul. He focused on his personal relationship with God and stayed close to Him throughout each day. He now keeps the possibilities, not the impossibilities, close to heart. God fills him, encourages him, and empowers him each day. The time of tearing down has ended, and God is rebuilding Robbie's life.

Are you allowing God to pour His life into you?

Today's Choice: Read Ecclesiastes 3:1–8. For each "time" Solomon lists (for example, time to plant and time to uproot) list at least one instance from your life that fits the category. Thank God for each of those events, then express your confidence that He'll bring you through to the other side of your current painful season too.

Reflections:

_____

_____

_____

_____

_____

What Should I Do?

Let the peace of Christ rule in your hearts, since as members of one body you were called to peace. And be thankful.

—Colossians 3:15

Sometimes when life rolls along peacefully, I wonder about struggles that may lie ahead. Depending on the severity of what shows up next, I can become emotionally and spiritually exhausted.

Here's the good news: the right response to a crisis can be spiritually, emotionally, and physically good for me. But when trouble comes, I still may say, "Really, God?" I'd rather be comfortable than challenged.

Various crises arrive on a regular basis: finances, occupation, family, marriage, church life, or health. Ephesians 1:11–12 says, "In him we were also chosen, having been predestined according to the plan of him who works out everything in conformity with the purpose of his will, in order that we, who were the first to put our hope in Christ, might be for the praise of his glory." God has planned out the details of our lives and incorporates them into His providential plan to make us more like His Son. This includes the crisis of a loved one identifying somewhere in the LGBTQ+ alphabet banner.

We may try to avoid reality by wallowing in denial, but we'll never move forward if we remain in that quicksand. Instead, consider how God wants you to navigate this crisis. You may be tempted to run away, searching for a place where you don't hear any more bad news. Or maybe you're tempted to manipulate the situation, trying to get the results you want instead of what God may desire.

Scripture presents two important realities about life. First, no matter what we do or how we live, some crises are going to sucker-punch us. We live in a sin-cursed world, and the Enemy of our soul hates us and will do everything possible to discourage our walk and drive us away from God. If we allow the Enemy to do that, we suffer and he celebrates.

Faith is a precious gift from God that will carry you through a crisis. Colossians 3:15 says, "Let the peace of God rule in your hearts." Whether the crisis is completely out of your hands or some portion is marginally under your control, ultimately you must trust God to show up and provide peace.

Dare to look your crisis in the eye and believe that God will take care of you, hear your prayers, and meet your every need. His peace is available if you allow Him access.

Today's Choice: Read Colossians 3:15–17. What do you see as the relationship between accessing God's peace and choosing to be thankful?

Reflections:

_____

_____

_____

_____

_____

Courage to Continue

*I have labored and toiled and have often gone without sleep; I have known hunger
and thirst and have often gone without food; I have been cold and naked.*

—2 CORINTHIANS 11:27

The roller coaster of emotions and situations that LGBTQ+ family
members ride is disorienting and frightening, especially if we feel
trapped. The coaster climbs and plummets, speeds up and slows down. Some
days we'd do almost anything to make the ride stop, unlock the lap bar, and
climb out of the cart.

But does walking away fit who God says we are? Does giving up show a
lack of courage to face what God is doing in our life? You may reasonably say,
"I don't want to do this, and I don't have to live like this or see my family hurt
over and over again."

The apostle Paul persevered because he knew God was with him and had
given him a job to do. Do you claim those truths in your tough times? Jewish
and Gentile opponents tried to capture and kill Paul on many occasions, but
he continued to praise God. The awareness of God's presence and calling
helped Paul endure beatings, imprisonments, and shipwrecks.

What was the source of his strength?

Paul trusted that he was right where God wanted him to be—even in
prison. He didn't indulge in self-pity or complaints, and he didn't waste his
time. He wrote letters of encouragement and counsel in his cell. He wit-
nessed to prison guards and others who visited him.

The apostle's example of faith and productivity in his trials encourages
us too. The same strength and faith are available to us through the Holy
Spirit. He can empower us to do what God tells us to do. But we, like Paul,
must claim the power and courageously continue onward. Our days will
flow much better when we begin the morning knowing God is with us, in
us, and for us.

Difficult circumstances humble us into admitting that without Christ Jesus we are weak, but with Him we are strong. Feeling inadequate to face reality prompts us to depend on God. He does not call the equipped; rather, He equips us to continue in the courage He offers us. We may not understand how any good will come from our situation, but we can trust God anyway. He may permit circumstances we don't want so He can reveal His faithfulness.

Paul knew he was doing what the Father called him to do. Think about what you're doing, how you're handling sleepless nights, the hunger for your loved one to come to God, and the roller-coaster emotions. Like Paul, are you willing to endure the suffering as you claim the strength of the Holy Spirit?

Today's Choice: Read 2 Corinthians 11:16–33. Paul is defending his apostleship in this passage by listing what he has been willing to suffer so he could preach the gospel. Think carefully about what hardships you're willing to endure so you can be a testimony to your loved one and others, then talk honestly with God about what He may be asking you to do.

Reflections:

_____

_____

_____

_____

_____

Overcoming Doubt

Then Jesus told him, "Because you have seen me, you have believed;
blessed are those who have not seen and yet have believed."

—JOHN 20:29

On some days Mary believed with all her heart that God was listening to her prayers and would give the healing and peace she desperately needed. She remained confident God would deliver her out of her circumstances.

Other days, though, the rumbling of ifs, whens, and whys knocked her to the ground. Those times of doubt didn't fit with what she knew in her head to be true. She began to see herself as a doubting Thomas—the disciple who said, "Unless I see the nail marks in his hands and put my finger where the nails were, and put my hand into his side, I will not believe [Jesus has risen from the dead]" (John 20:25).

The Enemy uses doubt to open the door to shame. Maybe God won't keep His promises if we doubt. Maybe He will ignore our prayers. The Enemy also uses doubt to drive us away from God. Questions and fears pile up, creating a barrier between God and us. If we allow that pile to grow until it towers over us like a skyscraper, we may even walk away from God.

Here's the truth about Thomas: Jesus reached out to him in spite of his doubt. Jesus said, "Put your finger here; see my hands. Reach out your hand and put it into my side. Stop doubting and believe" (John 20:27). Jesus says the same thing to you and me when we doubt: "Don't run away. Don't hide. Don't allow the Enemy to shame you. Come to me so I can remove your doubt."

God knows that our emotions and experiences can build our trust in Him; He also knows Satan can use those things to shatter us if our faith is not securely anchored in the facts about our risen Savior. Even in his doubt,

Thomas gathered together with the other disciples—that one step of faith initiated his amazing encounter with Jesus.

We may wish we had the opportunity, like Thomas, to dispel our doubt forever with a face-to-face encounter with Jesus. I think Jesus knew we'd feel that way, so He reached out to us with these words: "Blessed are those who have not seen [me], and yet have believed" (John 20:29).

Just as the father of the demon-possessed son cried out to Jesus in Mark 9:24, Mary learned to cry out to Him when doubts arose: "Help me overcome my unbelief!" You can reach out to Him that same way. And He will respond to you just as surely as He reached out to Thomas.

Today's Choice: Read John 20:24–29. How did Thomas respond when Jesus reached out to him? What do you think that statement signified? Are you willing to make that declaration too?

Reflections:

_____

_____

_____

_____

_____

Memorize the Word of God

The precepts of the Lord are right, rejoicing the heart; the commandment of the Lord is pure, enlightening the eyes . . . . the rules of the Lord are true, and righteous altogether. More to be desired are they than gold, even much fine gold; sweeter also than honey and drippings of the honeycomb.

—Psalm 19: 8–10 (ESV)

Sophia's life turned upside down and inside out the day her father left her mother to become a "she." She'd thought her family was normal—like her friends' families. Sure, her parents fought at times, but the fighting didn't seem to last long and generally their disagreements centered on Sophia or her brother. But this? How could her dad think he was female?

SAT testing was less than a week away, but all Sophia could think about was how Dad's decision would affect her and her brother when their friends found out what their father had done.

Her heart ached when she imagined her dad coming to see her looking like a woman. Anger burned inside her. How could he leave her mother after twenty-one years of marriage? She had even supported the family financially when he went back to college to get his PhD. How could he be so selfish—chasing this fantasy and tossing them aside as if they mean nothing to him?

Sophia knew she should talk to God about her anger and hurt feelings, but how could she know what God wanted to say to her? He wasn't going to come down from heaven and have lunch with her. Then she remembered her aunt sharing how much God's Word and memorizing Scripture helped her when her husband became paralyzed. She reached for her Bible on her bedside table and opened it to Psalm 19—a passage her youth director, Justin, had talked about the previous Sunday.

In Psalm 19, David wrote about how God's Word provided wisdom and comfort, joy and direction. Justin said that memorizing Bible verses can help us pull God into our circumstances. Whatever we're feeling, there's a Bible verse that speaks to that emotion. Scripture reminds us of God's presence and faithfulness and can sustain us in our pain, weariness, and uncertainty. David said God's Word was more valuable than money, more satisfying than honey.

We eat healthy food to ensure that our bodies and minds are strong. Scripture is food for the soul, and meditating on it exercises our faith muscles. Sophia followed her aunt's example and began to memorize Scripture. She started by writing out Psalm 19:8–10 on a sticky note and taping it to the bathroom mirror. She was amazed at how the reminder of God's truth helped her gain confidence in His ability to help their family.

Today's Choice: Read Psalm 19:7–14. What is your greatest need today—joy, wisdom, confidence? Find a verse that speaks to that need, write it down, and post it where you will see it several times a day. Memorize that verse, and the Holy Spirit will bring it to mind every time you need it.

Reflections:

_____

_____

_____

_____

_____

I Won't Back Down

Jesus said, "Father, if you are willing, take this cup from me;
yet not my will, but yours be done."

—LUKE 22:42

As I drove home the other day, an upbeat tune about not being pressured to conform to other people's standards came on the radio. Those of us with loved ones caught in the alphabet of LGBTQ+ have to make that commitment every day: I won't back down from God being my God. I won't back down from the guidelines He's given in Scripture.

Sooner or later, our faith is tested. At the beginning of His three years of ministry on earth, Jesus' faith was tested through the temptations of Satan (Matthew 4:1–11). On the night Jesus was betrayed by Judas, Jesus was in so much anguish that He sweat drops of blood (Luke 22:44). So why do we think we'll sail through life untested?

We can smile and play the Christian game pretending our lives are perfect, acting happy while we are dying inside. We can also charge ahead with our own agenda because God isn't moving fast enough or doing things our way. But maybe God has brought us to this difficult place because we need to learn that we cannot rely on our own wisdom.

Obedience is costly. Part of the cost is going through situations that force us to persevere so our faith grows stronger. When Jesus and the disciples went to the Mount of Olives the night before He was crucified, He said to them, "Pray that you will not fall into temptation" (Luke 22:40). But they didn't pray. They slept.

Jesus, on the other hand, walked a little further, knelt down, and prayed. He didn't want to drink the cup of suffering that lay ahead, but He was willing to submit to His Father's will—no matter how much it hurt.

Like me, you've probably prayed, "Take this cup from me." We don't want to drink the cup of suffering that a loved one's LGBTQ+ lifestyle brings.

Even though Jesus asked for a different outcome, He didn't waver in His faith or shy away from the job God had for Him because of the love He has for each of us. He did not back down. He stood His ground—no matter the cost. And "an angel from heaven appeared to him and strengthened him" (Luke 22:43).

If we pray in our anguish as Jesus did, God will help us resist the temptation of backing away from Him. We can stand our ground on the love that has been proven through the sacrifice of Jesus Christ. And He will send His angels—seen and unseen—to strengthen us.

Today's Choice: Read Luke 22:39–46. Ask God to supply the strength you need today to stand firm in your faith. Ask Him to show you how His angels are watching over you and ministering to you.

Reflections:

_____

_____

_____

_____

_____

Steady Hands

But Moses' hands became heavy; so they took a stone and put it under him, and he sat on it. And Aaron and Hur supported his hands, one on one side, and the other on the other side; and his hands were steady until the going down of the sun.

—Exodus 17:12 (NKJV)

If you look in the mirror and wonder how you can make it through another day, you aren't alone. As circumstances become more difficult or linger longer than you expected, your mind, body, and soul become weary. That's how Grandma Lori and Grandpa Bob felt when they received a wedding invitation from their granddaughter Patricia. At first, they had difficulty sleeping because they didn't know how to answer their precious granddaughter. They felt alone and unsteady.

Perhaps you've experienced some unsteadiness in your journey. The weight of family conflict and hard decisions may lie heavy on your heart too. What can you do? Ask God to send support as he sent support for Moses.

Moses and the army of Israel had to fight off the Amalekite army. Joshua led the troops into battle. Moses held up his rod. Then, when his arms grew heavy, Aaron and Hur kept Moses' hands lifted, so the Israelite army prevailed.

Moses could not prevail alone. Neither can you. Ask others for help in your battles and offer your help to them. Grandpa Bob and Grandma Lori found their support through the Word of God and through a visit with their pastor. They then wrote a loving letter to Patricia, confirming their love for her and her partner despite their conflicting views on human relationships and marriage. They assured her their love for her was unconditional—not based on what she did or didn't do. They didn't approve of her decision to marry her partner and wouldn't attend the ceremony, but their love for her wouldn't change.

If you wrestle with a challenge, go to God in private prayer and ask for His direction. You may grow weary, as Moses did, perhaps because spiritual battles are more difficult than physical ones. But as you cry out to God for supernatural strength, He will provide it.

The Spirit of God, who is our helper, can enable us to continue with our hands steady "until the going down of the sun"—until the evening of life is over and we witness the rising of the sun in a better land where prayer is swallowed up in praise.

Next time you wonder how you will make it through one more day—or maybe one more hour—close your eyes and envision your faith holding up one arm and hope holding up the other. You are sitting on the Rock of our salvation. Persevere and prevail.

Today's Choice: Read Exodus 17:8–15. Who or what has God sent to support you recently? How can you offer support to someone else?

Reflections:

_____

_____

_____

_____

_____

Choose to Trust

Not only so, but we also glory in our sufferings,
because we know that suffering produces perseverance.

—Romans 5:3

Angela had grown tired of attempting to find some level of normal in her life, let alone believing she'd ever feel joy and laugh again.

Her daughter, Stephanie, had chosen a path that led her into porn addiction mixed with homosexuality. Several times Stephanie's siblings had shared with Angela the cycle of girlfriends who entered and exited Stephanie's life. The relationship cycle seemed endless as did the porn addiction that had begun in high school.

Stephanie's lifestyle was so distant from God's best that Angela felt hopeless. She asked, "How do I persevere when I feel weak, hopeless, and ready to give up?" The years had eaten away at her hope and heart as did the locusts God sent the Egyptians because they wouldn't let the children of Israel go. The locusts covered "all the ground until it was black. . . . Nothing green remained on tree or plant in all the land of Egypt" (Exodus 10:15). That's how devastated Angela felt. The LGBTQ+ lifestyle was like a swarm of locusts. It had not only eaten up the daughter she'd known, but also her heart and her dreams for Stephanie.

Desperate, Angela knelt on the floor, and yelled at God, releasing a flood of tears. "Help me! Help me!" she sobbed.

When she finally calmed down and wiped her tears, she said, "I heard a voice, and my spirit quickened. Then I heard 'Will you trust Me?' My spirit and heart realized immediately it was not my imagination. It was my Lord who met me there on the floor."

Angela had a choice: she could trust God, or she could abandon hope, harden her heart, and cast aside her faith. She chose to trust God. And as her trust in Him grew, she exchanged unbelief and despair for belief and hope.

Satan will try to discourage us just as he discouraged Angela. He uses grief to keep our hearts heavy and disappointment to drown our hopes. He whispers lies about your circumstances and healing being impossible.

When you feel like giving up, ask yourself, "Do I serve an almighty, powerful, loving God or a god that is dead?" If you choose the living God as He is revealed in the Bible, then stop digging the hole of doubt Satan wants to bury you in.

Focus on what you know to be true about God. Stay away from everything that shifts your focus away from Him. Trust Him to lead you—maybe even carry you—through each minute of each day. Don't give up.

Today's Choice: Read Romans 5:1–5. What is the hope that cannot be taken from us? How does that hope fuel your ability to trust God?

Reflections:

_____

_____

_____

_____

_____

When Your Situation
Seems Impossible

When Abram was ninety-nine years old, the Lord appeared to him and said,
"I am God Almighty; walk before me faithfully."

—GENESIS 17:1

E ver feel like you've been trapped in a maze that has no exit?

When we face the heartbreak of a loved one's decision to pursue an LGBTQ+ lifestyle, we can feel so lost and disoriented that we say, "There's no way out of this!"

Take heart. The Lord loves to do the impossible. Think of Abraham, who left Ur of the Chaldeans and moved to a faraway country, where warlords were ready to kill him and steal his flocks. Abraham set up house in that land anyway, built altars, and worshiped God because he put his trust in God, not in his circumstances (Genesis 12:4–9).

Abraham also believed that God would fulfill His promise of an heir— even though Abraham was ninety-nine and his wife, Sarah, was eighty-nine. God assured Abraham, "I will bless [Sarah], and will surely give you a son by her . . . so that she will be the mother of nations; kings of peoples will come from her" (Genesis 17:16). One year later, Abraham and Sarah celebrated the birth of their son, Isaac (Genesis 21:1–2).

The impossible turned into the possible because God willed it. Scripture tells us, "Against all hope, Abraham in hope believed and so became the father of many nations" (Romans 4:18). When we, like Abraham, surrender ourselves to the map, journey, and destination God has set before us, we too are able to hope "against all hope" that He will do the impossible for us and our family.

Abraham had questions about God's plan just as we do, and sometimes he took matters into his own hands just as we do. God didn't explain everything to Abraham, and He won't answer all our questions either. But we, like Abraham, can cultivate a pattern of trust and obedience, which God will reward in His time. Abraham and Sarah waited twenty-five years for the birth of Isaac, the heir God had promised them. You may have to wait a long while for God's perfect time too.

In the meantime, don't sit and sulk. Travel the road God has laid out before you even if it seems impossible to take one more step. Be open to what God does want to do; don't focus on what seems impossible for Him to accomplish.

The Lord may lead you, like Abraham, into impossible situations so He can demonstrate His great power. Eventually, He will lead you out of the maze, and you will celebrate as Abraham and Sarah celebrated: "God has brought me laughter [joy], and everyone who hears about this will laugh with me" (Genesis 21:6).

Today's Choice: Abraham and Sarah's story is recorded in Genesis 12–18, 20–24. Read as much of their story as you can over the next few days. When was their faith strong? When was it weak? How did God reveal His faithfulness all along their journey? Then think back over the last few months and jot down examples of God's faithfulness.

Reflections:

_____

_____

_____

_____

_____

Setting Boundaries

And the Lord God commanded the man, "You are free to eat from any tree in the garden; but you must not eat from the tree of the knowledge of good and evil, for when you eat of it you will certainly die."

—GENESIS 2:16–17

F amily members usually struggle to set boundaries for their LGBTQ+ loved ones. Parents struggle with what they should allow in their home and how they should interact with their child in other settings. Children ask themselves, "Do I want a relationship at this time with my parent?" Spouses whose marriages have crumbled wonder how to handle social gatherings with friends and extended family. Grandparents face similar decisions regarding children and grandchildren.

One wife said, "In my struggle with the idea of boundaries, I found myself torn between knowing I couldn't (and shouldn't) tolerate my husband's sin and a belief that taking action would be selfish and unloving. Each time a new discovery of his acting out came to light, I clearly communicated to him that it wasn't okay, but beyond that, I didn't know what to do. I felt so helpless."

Like this woman, we don't want to ostracize our LGBTQ+ loved one. But when that person pursues destructive behaviors or creates conflict in the family, we can set limits to prevent the Enemy from taking us down and to allow God space to bring healing.

Boundaries are rooted in the nature of God. He gave Adam and Eve the freedom to live within His boundaries or outside of them. When they chose to disregard His boundaries, they faced the consequences. Similarly, if we or our loved ones choose to step outside of God's boundaries, we must accept the consequences.

When we honor God's boundaries in our lives and relationships, we communicate where the actions of our loved one will reach the extent of our tolerance and where they must honor our convictions. Boundaries establish who we are as children of God—our allegiance to Him and our desire to honor Him in all our relationships. Boundaries define our safe zone—like a cabin in the woods limits where bears and wildcats roam. Boundaries also limit destructive behaviors and allow us time to restore balance and perspective, to move forward, and to heal.

A person with no boundaries is undefined and unprotected. The result is confusion—for the family member and the LGBTQ+ loved one. We won't know how to proceed when we feel violated, because we won't know for sure that we have been violated. Neither will our loved one.

Instead of viewing boundaries as unloving and intolerant, ponder the goodness of the boundaries set by God in His relationship with us, then apply those boundaries to your relationship with others.

Today's Choice: Read Genesis 3. What boundaries did God set for Adam and Eve? Why were they good boundaries? What were the consequences of disobeying those boundaries?

Reflections:

_____

_____

_____

_____

_____

Worthy of Being Loved

So that Christ may dwell in your hearts through faith; and that you, being rooted and grounded in love may be able to comprehend with all the saints what is the width and length and height and depth, and to know the love of Christ which surpasses knowledge, that you may be filled to all the fullness of God.

—Ephesians 3:17–19 (NASB)

Like me, you probably try hard to be good and perfect in your walk with Jesus. But no matter how hard we work, life happens and sends our emotions, reactions, and behaviors into a sinful spiral. I can attempt to be the perfect daughter, wife, mother, grandmother, and friend. But sooner or later, I will fail someone.

When we're confronted with our failure and its fruit, we may feel like an utter failure. We may feel that we aren't doing enough, or somehow we aren't enough in and of ourselves. For days, months, maybe even years we consider our life a failure because we were unable to stop our loved one from walking away from God.

Perhaps nothing seems to be going right, or perhaps in a moment of weakness, we really blew it and did something we knew to be wrong. Our own feeling-less-than labels are damaging enough. But the Enemy of our souls loves to add his own labels by reminding us of past failures, including ones long forgiven and forgotten. He prompts us to replay past failures of not being the perfect child, spouse, parent, friend, or representative of God's family.

Feelings of unworthiness will visit us from time to time just like an unwanted visit from an overly critical neighbor or relative. The Enemy uses these feelings of failure and inadequacy to steal our joy, particularly when we equate them with being unworthy of God's love.

God welcomed us into His family with full knowledge of everything we would ever do or fail to do. We can't impress God with our goodness.

No matter how hard we try to do right, we will fail and need His forgiveness and grace. What we may consider to be our most righteous acts are so far from His standard of holiness that they are as "filthy rags" in His sight (Isaiah 64:6).

The good news is that Jesus' death and resurrection changes everything! In Christ, we are clothed in His robes of righteousness. We stand before Him unashamed, not because we are pure but because He is pure. He has made us worthy.

The next time you feel unworthy to go before throne of God, remember that in your robe of Jesus' righteousness, you have 24/7 access to Him. God loves you and accepts you because of Christ's sacrifice on the cross. Neither your past, present, nor future failures affect your position of beloved acceptance as a child of God. Rejoice!

Today's Choice: Read Paul's prayer in Ephesians 3:14–20. Why do you think being "rooted and established in love" is essential to accessing the power Paul speaks of? How is the knowledge of God's love for us related to the knowledge of everything else about Him?

Reflections:

_____

_____

_____

_____

_____

Claim Victory As You Wait

But those who wait on the Lord shall renew their strength; they shall mount up with wings as eagles; they shall run and not be weary; they shall walk and not faint.

—Isaiah 40:31 (NKJV)

God often uses waiting as a crucible in which to refine our character. Perhaps the prophet Isaiah realized this when he wrote about the benefits of waiting expectantly for God to act.

Waiting on God to direct our steps or meet a need makes us stronger, not weaker. He's not asking us to sit around tapping our foot until something happens; rather, we should remain attentive and quiet, listening for His voice and watching intently for evidence of His movement in our lives and circumstances.

Many who read these words are facing situations that appear hopeless. You feel like God isn't listening to your prayers because your predicament seems unchanged. But waiting for God to tend to your needs and your loved one's needs is one of the most beneficial spiritual practices.

For example, after a phone conversation with a woman named Lynn ended, I asked the Lord to show her how to live a life of victory despite her circumstances. Her son, who was transitioning to female, was engaged to a young woman who planned to transition to male. Lynn's son intended to wear a wedding gown, and his fiancée a tux. Just when Lynn thought she heard all her heart could bear, the couple announced they intended to adopt children when they felt ready.

Claiming victory in such a situation can seem impossible. But Lynn is learning to wait faithfully on God. Daily, she sets aside worry and hopelessness; she's committed to trust God and persevere until He acts.

If we don't regularly ask God to fill our cup of hope, we begin to lose hope. Spiritual transformation doesn't take place immediately; it is forged in us while we're waiting, hoping, and trusting. As we wait, we can rest in the knowledge that God doesn't ask us to do anything He hasn't already done. God has, in fact, field-tested waiting and given us the perfect example to follow in Jesus Christ.

When we continue to place our trust in God and in His schedule—not ours—we develop the long-range perspective that allows Him to renew our strength so we can "run, and not be weary . . . walk, and not faint."

Meditate on all the possibilities available to our almighty, loving God. Continue to trust Him to answer your prayers and accomplish His will. Sing songs of praise for what He has promised. He is bringing His plan to completion in His time.

Today's Choice: Read Isaiah 40:6–31. What does Isaiah emphasize about humans and about God? Which of the truths he lists about God are most meaningful to you today? Why?

Reflections:

_____

_____

_____

_____

_____

Encounter God
through Journaling

Trust in him at all times, you people; pour out your hearts to him,
for God is our refuge.

—Psalm 62:8

As a child, I had a small diary with a key. When I faced difficult days, I entered the date and expressed my heart. If I had a good day with Dad, I wrote about it. After I put all my thoughts in writing, I locked the diary and hid it. Sometimes when I pulled it out again, I read what I wrote days or months ago. Writing about current situations and reading about previous circumstances helped me stay focused on God and reminded me of how He was present with me in my journey. I still journal today.

Perhaps you think you're too busy to add one more task to your to-do list. But when it comes to healing, we should make time to care for ourselves. Putting pen to paper or fingers to keyboard provides healing for both men and women.

As the psalmist suggests, start by pouring out your heart to God. Write honestly. On the rough days, writing will help you process your pain. Also record any sign that God is working: a change in your loved one's attitude or your positive reaction to a hurtful comment or action.

Here are some examples of honest journal entries:

> *Theresa:* Dear God, How did I get here? Ten months of what feels like a taste of hell. My body has been shocked, and every cell in my body has been attacked. I confess before You, I am a mother gasping for air, and flat before Your feet. I feel empty, dried up and dead. All that's left is a shell of my body. My heart bled out, leaving me where I am, joyless, and filled with sorrow.

Mark: Father, I've done the best I was able. But it doesn't seem like my best was good enough. I feel like I've failed my son most of all. Though I need to be the strong one to hold my family together, I feel weak all through my body. I need You, Lord, please minister to my heart and guide me through this journey.

Cathy: Dear God, it's been over two years of walking this difficult journey with my daughter. I am encouraged on the days I hear or see my daughter. When she smiles, I feel happiness. But I feel discouragement when I see her facial reactions when I share anything of my life revolving around You and church. I fear what she may think of You or how she feels about You. I know I don't see her heart as You do, Lord, so please keep me from judging what I see on the outside and remember You are in the inside calling out to her.

Don't sugarcoat your feelings or edit your diary entries. Write what's true and real. Ask God to give you the courage to write the truth and expect that, as you do, God will meet you where you are and help you grow.

Today's Choice: Like the writer of Psalm 62, Hannah poured out her heart to God in 1 Samuel 1:10. Verse eighteen says that "her face was no longer downcast." Why do you think pouring out her heart helped her? How does it help you?

Reflections:

_____

_____

_____

_____

_____

Praising God Brings Healing

I will exalt you, my God the King; I will praise your name for ever and ever.
Every day I will praise you and extol your name for ever and ever.

—Psalm 145:1–2

One way to enter a place of trust and faith is praise and worship. God yearns for His people to praise Him, but often we are so focused on our hurt and difficult circumstances that we don't use one of the most healing tools available to us—praise!

You may be thinking, *She must be kidding. How can I praise God when I'm in such pain?*

I've had similar thoughts, but I chose to praise God anyway. I was amazed by its transforming power—especially when I don't feel like doing it. When we are weighed down by stress and discouragement, the Enemy tries to destroy our faith in God's promises and our hope. But when we worship through praise songs, we discover God is the shield that protects us from the Enemy and God is the balm for our hurting heart.

Through music, we are literally praying with our heart, soul, and spirit. The result is always an impartation of God's infinite blessings, wisdom, knowledge, and understanding. When we focus on who God is, we can more easily trust Him to take care of our loved ones and bring them back to His loving embrace.

Worship is more than thankfulness for what God has done. It's praising God for who He is without asking questions or seeking answers. Worship is submitting to God, so we can enter His presence with an obedient, humble heart and receive refuge, strength, and healing.

A treasured hymn I sing often is "Amazing Grace." The words always calm me and help me refocus on God's goodness. When I'm home alone, worshiping through music and dancing becomes a tender time of fellowship between me and God. As I dance, joy seems to burst into my heart, and I feel so connected to the One who loves me.

God wants to shower us with an outpouring of His miraculous healing and blessings. Praise and worship can help us draw closer to Him. And, for me, the louder I sing and the more I move, the closer I feel to Him.

When we use the psalms to praise God, our body, mind, and soul come into alignment with His Word. Through praise and worship, we step deeper into faith. And through our faith, God's healing Spirit is able to work within us.

Offer Him the sacrifice of praise, thanksgiving, and joy and see what He does in your life. I believe you will experience a closeness that brings healing for your heart and soul.

Today's Choice: Read Psalm 145. Choose a familiar tune and sing verses 8–20 back to God. Sing loud, lift your hands heavenward, and dance!

Reflections:

_____

_____

_____

_____

_____

Tell Yourself the Truth

But this I call to mind, and therefore I have hope; The steadfast love of the Lord never ceases; his mercies never come to an end; they are new every morning; great is your faithfulness. "The Lord is my portion," says my soul, "therefore I will hope in him."

—LAMENTATIONS 3:21–24 (ESV)

Sarah woke up feeling ill the day after her son Travis announced he was going to marry his old girlfriend from college and planned to transition. Travis said he had full support from his girlfriend, Jeannie.

"I felt like I'd been hit in the gut with a soccer ball," she later said. "Where did this begin and what happened to our son?"

Kenny, Sarah's husband, was going on an out-of-town business trip the next day. She wondered how on earth he could conduct business meetings. "We'll never survive this," she muttered. Travis's news was too much for either of them to handle, and neither wanted to face the truth.

But ignoring the facts didn't help. Soon both Kenny and Sarah were stressed, irritable, and distraught. Their relationship with each other deteriorated because they no longer connected emotionally; burying the truth created a path to go their separate ways, absorbed in their own feelings and pain.

In the book of Lamentations, the prophet Jeremiah wrote honestly about his feelings. He had watched an enemy army destroy Jerusalem and kill many Jews. Like Travis's parents, he felt hopeless. Jeremiah lamented over the people's sin and God's subsequent judgment. The prophet voiced his despair and shared his pain just as you likely have. But he didn't stay in that pit. He also reminded himself of the truth he knew—God was faithful.

When we face the truth about our circumstances and our feelings, we allow God the opportunity to be our helper. Difficult circumstances don't have to destroy our human relationships. If we focus on God's faithfulness and unconditional love, our relationship with Him and with others can grow stronger.

Sarah and Kenny decided to talk honestly about Travis and his plans. The situation was not going to disappear; in fact, it would surely become more challenging. Speaking truthfully also enabled them to process their feelings and support each other.

Like Sarah and Kenny, you have a choice. You can stay in the unhappiness of your circumstances and allow them to control you and destroy all those around you, or you can remind yourself of who God is, what He has done, and what He promises to do.

When you find yourself thinking *I'll never survive this*, speak the truth. It's okay to talk honestly about where you are today, but God doesn't expect you to stay where you are. Instead, He wants you to push through, knowing He's got your back no matter how tough it may be today.

Today's Choice: Read Lamentations 3:1–26. In what ways do you identify with Jeremiah's questions and feelings? What evidence of God's steadfast love and faithfulness do you see in your life right now?

Reflections:

_____

_____

_____

_____

_____

The Omnipotence of God

Ah, Sovereign Lord, you have made the heavens and the earth by your great
power and outstretched arm. Nothing is too hard for you.

—Jeremiah 32:17

What part of your journey today seems "too hard" for God? The Enemy wants us to believe that God can't—or won't—fix this or that aspect of our situation. We may be willing to trust God in most areas, but not in this one area.

With the help of the Holy Spirit, though, and daily time in the Word of God and prayer, you will be able to release that one area to God—just as Levi did.

Levi believed God couldn't reach his daughter, Tammy. He knew she was suffering deep grief in her lesbian relationships. And then Tammy shared her plans to have a baby with her current partner. Levi felt buried alive in his grief-stricken heart—not only for his daughter but also for the child to be born into this environment.

Feeling hopeless, he struggled when well-meaning folks asked about Tammy. Friends at work and church shared their parental struggles with him, but no one seemed to be in the same situation as he was, or they were ashamed to mention it if they were.

Levi could have yelled at God and turned away from Him with an angry, broken heart. Instead, Levi's helplessness motivated him to rely on God's sovereignty and omnipotence in the messy relationship with his daughter, her partner, and the child they would raise. Placing the situation into God's capable hands—and leaving it there—deepened Levi's relationship and dependency on Him.

In a wobbly step of faith, Levi chose to let go of his disbelief and trust God to be who He says He is. Instead of living in grief, Levi discovered a life of peace as he let go of Tammy—whom he'd made his idol by allowing her to control his life rather than God. He committed her to God, saying, "Do whatever You must, Lord, to work things out for the glory of Your kingdom."

Today Levi is living in hope, believing that God will work a miracle for Tammy and his grandchild yet to come.

You can choose to live that way too. Let go of the "too hard" mindset and offer this prayer to the God who loves you and your loved one more than you can imagine:

Dear heavenly Father, I know I've not always trusted You completely. I've held back and doubted Your sovereignty. Forgive me. I cannot handle my situation alone. Help my faith in You to grow and come alive in a way that helps me live in joy and hope, no matter my circumstances. Nothing is too hard for You! In Jesus' name, amen.

Today's Choice: Read Jeremiah 32. How does Jeremiah express both his confusion and his faith in vv. 17–25? What is God's response in verses 26–42? Try to express both your confusion and faith to God today, then listen for His response.

Reflections:

_____

_____

_____

_____

_____

Make Health a Priority

And so, dear brothers and sisters, I plead with you to give your bodies to God because of all he has done for you. Let them be a living and holy sacrifice—the kind he will find acceptable. This is truly the way to worship him, for you were bought with a price. So glorify God in your bodies.

—Romans 12:1 (NLT)

O ur body is a gift from God, and we should take care of it. But the stress of having an LGBTQ+ loved one wears us down mentally, emotionally, and physically whether we are the parent, spouse, child, other relative, or close friend.

On this journey, we can become so self-focused on what we're going through that taking care of our body just doesn't seem important. Our energy level may also be extremely low due to lack of proper nutrition or sleep.

You may recognize your need for spiritual nourishment and invest extra time in prayer, Bible study, counseling, or worship. But your body needs energy for those activities too. If you're not caring for your physical needs, you may feel increasingly lethargic, which makes it more difficult to do anything beneficial.

Have you found yourself lying on the couch or bed, saying, "I can't get up, nor do I want to"? On those days, you may want to blame your LGBTQ+ loved one or the circumstances that have arisen from their decisions. But the truth is, you've permitted your loved one or circumstances to control you and affect your well-being. Passing the blame to someone or something else is shirking your God-given responsibility to care for your body, mind, and soul.

If you're like me, stress motivates you to eat unhealthy foods—sugary drinks, salty snacks, candy, or maybe your favorite fast-food meal. A poor diet will only make you feel worse about yourself, and it may also hinder your desire to deal with the hidden heart issues that send you on those binges in the first place.

Paul tells us to give our body to God—a sacrificial act of worship that pleases Him. When we take care of our bodies, we demonstrate that we love God and are thankful for our bodies. If you're struggling to connect with God, He may be speaking to you about what you are actually putting in your body or what you are denying it (exercise and rest).

Be a good steward of your body. If you like to walk, walk. If there's a sport you enjoy—tennis, baseball, swimming—get back to doing it. If you need to change your eating habits, start by adding one healthy habit a week (water instead of soda or fruit instead of candy). Your circumstances should not control your health. Allow the Holy Spirit to help you take back control of your body.

Today's Choice: Read Romans 12:1–2. Think about the poor health patterns you've developed and ask God to renew your thinking about those habits and transform them one by one.

Reflections:

_____

_____

_____

_____

_____

Maintain a Godly Perspective

I have fought the good fight, I have finished the race, I have kept the faith.

—2 Timothy 4:7

Perspective is vital. How we live from here on out will either put us on the road to healing, hope, and wholeness or keep us captive to the negative thoughts and habits the Enemy uses against us.

Are you willing to exchange your current perspective for the faith-based perspective of all things are possible through God? Perspective is often more important than reality: we may not be able to change our circumstances, but we can always alter our perspective about them.

Seeing life from God's perspective instead of our own or someone else's is an ongoing challenge. The apostle Paul faced many challenges throughout his decades of ministry, and yet he maintained a godly perspective on his circumstances and their relationship to God's eternal plan.

In his second letter to young Pastor Timothy, Paul acknowledged that God had helped him stay faithful and strong, and he invited all followers of Christ to remain faithful and strong. Keeping the faith is like a fight and a race, he said, and we must persevere through pain to be the victor, to reach the finish line.

Paul also emphasized that our sinful nature works against us. We struggle with the tendency to trust ourselves and to believe we can fix our problems faster or better than God can.

Here's what others have shared about how they maintain a godly perspective:

> Cassie and James: "We pray God's promises over our son Jacob and continue to believe God will be faithful and bring our son back to Him. Because of God's faithfulness, we are living life with expectedness of great things for Jacob to come."

Amanda: "My husband left for the life he thought would bring him happiness. Though we are no longer married, I pray for God to intervene in his life and bring him healing. I choose to believe God will answer my prayers for him."

Ron: "I once lived a life of disbelief but found that led me to a dead end. Now I live a life of belief that God will do what He needs to do to bring my daughter back to her faith roots and into relationship with Him again. Because of this, I live a life of expectation."

We fight to stay focused on God, and we persevere through adversity to finish the race He has asked us to run. We've come too far to give up. Together, let's fight the fight, finish the race, and keep our faith!

Today's Choice: Read 2 Timothy 4:1–8. What challenge does Paul give Timothy? What warning does he give? What reward awaits those who finish their race?

Reflections:

_____

_____

_____

_____

_____

Exercising Your Faith

For physical training is of some value, but godliness has value for all things,
holding promise for both the present life and the life to come.

—1 TIMOTHY 4:8

Some journeys lead us to places we'd rather not go on a road we wish we'd never taken. God sometimes allows us to encounter challenges we cannot fix, obstacles that force us to move beyond our comfort zone. Confronting those challenges can be uncomfortable, especially if our muscles haven't been stretched in a while.

Our physical bodies need stretching to keep our muscles flexible, strong, and healthy. Stretching helps our muscles to maintain a range of motion. Without proper conditioning, our muscles contract and tighten, resulting in weakness and inflexibility that may result in muscle damage.

If we amble along on a straight, level path in life, we become comfortable, and our faith can lose its strength, flexibility, and resiliency. Challenges force us to strengthen those faith muscles. Flexing our spiritual muscles may hurt the first few days, just like physical muscles that are stretched in uncomfortable positions. But our heart will grow stronger, our will more flexible, and our attitude more resilient as we begin to see ourselves as God sees us and to view our circumstances as He views them.

Spiritual exercise will give the Holy Spirit an opportunity to cultivate godliness in us, which, Paul told Timothy, "has value for all things." The word translated "godliness" in 1 Timothy 4:8 refers to reverence and respect for God and His ways. Some Bible versions use the phrase "godly living" or "devotion to God" to describe this goal of spiritual training.

One way we can exercise our faith muscles is to look for God in our uncomfortable circumstances. He is far more present and active in our personal life than we may imagine. Look for Him in creation, in the encouragement of a friend, and in a song on the radio. He may even show up as you do a load of laundry or prepare a meal.

Prayer is also a way to condition our spiritual muscles. Our pain may be intense, but our heart still yearns to connect with God. We may be begging Him to reach out to our loved one, but He knows that our will needs to be aligned with His. Only He can speak and minister to us in a way that strengthens our faith muscles as they are stretched.

How well-conditioned are your faith muscles? Start a new training program today by looking for God in your circumstances and by spending more time in prayer conversations with Him.

Today's Choice: Read 1 Timothy 4:7–16 and 2 Timothy 2:15–16. What spiritual exercises does Paul recommend to young Pastor Timothy in these verses? How can you incorporate one or more of them into your daily routine?

Reflections:

_____

_____

_____

_____

_____

Take Care of Yourself

Or do you not know that your body is a temple of the Holy Spirit within you, whom you have from God? You are not your own, for you were bought with a price. So glorify God in your body.

—1 Corinthians 6:19–20 (ESV)

When Charlene heard that both her children were living a LGBTQ+ life, she became obsessively focused on how to help each one realize the life they were leading was far from being spiritually good for them.

The oldest, Samantha, had always seemed happy and well-rounded—school, sports, theater, and youth group—until she got involved with fellow classmate, Janey. Then Samantha's attitude changed. She became disrespectful, always looking for a fight with one or both parents.

Samantha's younger brother, Shane, wanted to be like his older sister. He spied on her and listened to her phone calls. Feeling invisible as a boy, he began to dress up in Samantha's clothing when no one was home.

Charlene and her husband, Jonathan, tried everything they could think of to influence their children. After many failed attempts, they felt empty. They battled depression, they stopped attending church, their job performance deteriorated, and Jonathan began to have health issues.

One day, when Charlene returned home early from work, she saw herself in a hallway mirror. Her skin was pale and her expression lifeless. She asked herself, "What have my children done to me?" Then she rephrased her question, "What have I done to myself?"

For the first time, she considered how she had allowed her children's lifestyles to affect her body, mind, and soul. She walked into the bathroom and picked up the depression medication her doctor had prescribed. She realized that she and her husband had to find a new way of handling their situation before it sucked any more of life from them.

When Jonathan came home, they talked about how desperately they needed to take care of their mental and physical health and, most importantly, their need to restore their relationship with God.

God expects us to take care of ourselves. He doesn't want us to neglect or misuse our bodies. Neglecting our health will never improve our situation; such abuse can only lead to sorrow and suffering, maybe even death.

When we accept Christ as Savior, God Himself comes to live within us by His Holy Spirit, and if we misuse our body, we are sinning against the Holy One who now lives within us. As 1 Corinthians 6:20 says, we bring glory to God by taking care of ourselves. Treat your body as the temple of the Holy Spirit. Care for it as if it were your most precious possession—because it is.

Today's Choice: Read Proverbs 3:5–8 and 1 Corinthians 6:18–20. According to these passages, how are mental, physical, and spiritual health interrelated? How well do you care for each facet of your being?

Reflections:

_____

_____

_____

_____

_____

The Gift of Peace

Jesus said, "Peace I leave with you; my peace I give you. I do not give to you as the world gives. Do not let your hearts be troubled and do not be afraid."

—JOHN 14:27

I n the beginning or middle of our journey, we may often cry out to God for peace. The ground and foundation of our faith, life, and family has been shaken. Our body cries out for rest, but it eludes us. Our soul and heart are dehydrated as we trudge through the desert of our circumstances. Peace seems like a mirage—we glimpse it on the horizon, then it vanishes before we reach it.

You may think that you'll only attain peace when your loved one, like the prodigal son, has come back home and life is back to normal—whatever that may be. Or perhaps you assume peace can be negotiated so everything aligns with your vision of life, and no conflict or difficulties arise.

But that's not how God's peace works. His peace can bring calmness in the middle of the chaos. Accessing His peace is connected to our confidence that He will help us complete the assignment or journey He's assigned us.

In the second part of John 14:27, Jesus says, "Do not let your hearts be troubled and do not be afraid." How is that possible when your world is crumbling around you and all seems hopeless? Jesus can say that to us because He has also promised that He and God the Father will make their home with us (John 14:23). If the Father and Son are with us, we have no reason to be afraid.

God's peace provides a refuge for us as we deal with life's issues and challenges. But peace is elusive because we tend to focus on everything else going on and forget the Father and the Son are working on our behalf every minute of every day. If we're distracted, we may forget who we serve and who is really in control—the all-powerful, all-loving God of the universe.

Place whatever is causing you anxiety and the outcome in God's hands. As you place more and more trust in Him, your anxiety will decrease and peace will increase.

Friends and family may not understand the peace you have, but they will notice it, which will give you the opportunity to testify of God's presence, provision, and protection. As you walk through trials, refuse to allow fear or worry to rule your thoughts and give God the opportunity to fill you with His peace.

Today's Choice: Read John 14:23–31. What do these verses teach us about those who experience God's peace? What habits do they cultivate? What truths about God do they embrace?

Reflections:

_____

_____

_____

_____

_____

Offering Kindness

*Be kind to one another, tenderhearted, forgiving one another,
as God in Christ forgave you.*

—Ephesians 4:32 (ESV)

Ephesians 4:32 offers three short but important commands. First,
Paul tells us to exhibit kindness. Second, Paul uses the Greek word
eusplanchnoi, which means "tenderhearted" or "compassionate." The focus is
showing sympathy for others and their circumstances.

Paul then gives a concrete example of what compassion looks like:
forgive one another. This instruction comes with an explanation, referring
to the forgiveness believers have received from Christ. He alone knows our
heart, and obedience calls us to forgive others as He forgives us. No matter
what hurt your loved one or others have inflicted on you, forgive them and
demonstrate a Christlike attitude of love and compassion.

Kindness brings healing to those who are hurting. Sacrificing our comfort for others and even taking some risks to help other people will diminish
our own pain. Extend kindness whenever possible, especially to the hurting.

When you face heart-wrenching situations that assault every cell in your
body, the chaos causes stress and anxiety for family members. Hard as it may
be to do at times, remaining calm is a first step. If you need to step out of the
room for a few moments or go for a walk, do it. Avoid reacting in ways you
may later regret.

Kindness isn't usually our initial reaction. We may seek payback or make
demands. When we react to situations with anger and emotional drama, the
negative cycle continues as long as you perpetuate it.

You may also be scared to find out what's behind your loved one's determination to embrace the LGBTQ+ lifestyle. Fear can generate guilt. You feel
guilty because you wish you'd handled situations differently, or you take on
the burden of the guilt you believe someone else has or should have. I have

done all of that. But my healing didn't begin until I unearthed the core of what was making me feel so guilty.

You may also think your loved one doesn't deserve your respect. When you're tempted to hurl accusations or judgments at him or her, remember you are God's ambassador. Treat your loved one respectfully and kindly—as God would. Give Him space and time to reach down deep into your loved one's heart, correct wayward behaviors, and draw them close.

Your loved one also has to desire help. He or she has issues to work through, just as you and I do. Showing kindness to those who hurt you is a step in the right direction.

Today's Choice: Read Ephesians 4:29–32. Ask God to reveal the unwholesome and unhelpful words you've spoken recently, then ask Him to show you how to show compassion to those who have hurt you.

Reflections:

_____

_____

_____

_____

_____

Continual Praise

Through him then let us continually offer up a sacrifice of praise to God, that is, the fruit of lips that acknowledge his name.

—Hebrews 13:15 (ESV)

Do you feel like praising God when you're angry, depressed, or hurting? Probably not. But praising God when we don't feel like it may be the shortest path out of those emotional pits.

The writer of the book of Hebrews calls praise a sacrifice, which indicates praise is an act of worship we offer God regardless of our emotional state.

Julie shares, "When I learned the truth of my daughter's life, I could barely get out of bed. I listened to sermons that suggested I should praise God, but I struggled to do it. Then one day I offered God a small praise. I praised Him for the sunshine. It was short and simple. The following day I praised Him for the sunshine and the blue skies. This was the beginning of taking my eyes off my pain and refocusing on God. Before long, I realized God was working in my heart, and the heaviness was in the beginning stages of lifting."

Julie started with thanksgiving for simple, daily blessings. Hebrews 13:15 also says that our praise should "acknowledge his name." When the Bible talks about God's name, it's referring to His character and His reputation. Even when everything about our life or our loved one's life seems terrible, we can praise God for who He is: wise, loving, and merciful.

Praising God when you don't feel like it is also an acknowledgment of His sovereignty, goodness, and trustworthiness. You're sacrificing your will and your emotions on the altar of submission to His worthiness to be praised. You're declaring in the midst of your pain, "Not my will but Yours, O Lord."

When you practice the spiritual discipline of sacrificial praise not only is God glorified, but your faith also grows stronger. Praise leads to blessings.

In being more focused on God than on ourselves, we step into His presence, which provides shelter from life's storms.

Many people find it helpful to name three praises before they get out of bed in the morning or before they go to sleep at night. Some keep a journal of daily praises. Find a technique that works for you and commit to it.

As Julie chose to give God her praise and turn her heart toward Him, He opened her eyes to more ways He was working in her heart. He will do the same for you.

Today's Choice: Read Hebrews 13:15–16. What else does the writer list as sacrifices that please God? How can those sacrifices help us discover more reasons to praise God?

Reflections:

_____

_____

_____

_____

_____

Releasing Control

The works of his hands are faithful and just; all his precepts are trustworthy.

—Psalm 111:7 (ESV)

Many of us struggle with releasing control to God because we believe that by hanging on, we have some sort of control over our journey's outcome. But the truth is, we have no control over a loved one identifying as LGBTQ+ or their decisions. The faster we acknowledge that truth, the faster we allow God to take over.

A balanced approach to dealing with hard situations is essential. We cannot maintain rigid standards or demands; neither can we be complacent or apathetic. Most important, we cannot be someone's savior. If we listen, we will probably hear the Holy Spirit say, "You aren't trusting Me like you say you do."

Some of us struggle with releasing control because we have trouble admitting our reality is what it is at this time and we are powerless to change it. However, the Lord wants us to repent from our self-centered need to control and lovingly hand over our need in exchange for His greatness.

Our struggle to release control is also a symptom of pride. Yielding to God forces us to admit our weaknesses and vulnerability. But we cannot grow strong in faith and truly honor God until we place everything in His hands.

When we admit our need to depend on God, He can replace our desperation with hope and place us on a path to deeper understanding of who He really is. The Enemy will attempt to implant in your mind negative and destructive thoughts about your situation. He doesn't want you to give God full control of your child, grandchild, parent, sibling, or friend. Refuse to give in to him and his messages any longer. Use God's Word to defend your mind against his attacks. The Enemy's power is limited, and he can't be in the presence of God's Word for long.

If, as the psalmist says, God is faithful and just, we can be confident that He will do what is best for us and for our loved ones. If all God's precepts—His rules for successful living—are trustworthy, then He will bring about the best results.

Step back and reflect on the greatness, wonder, and power of the God we serve. Think of Bible stories that illustrate His expert handling of difficult circumstances. Think of past situations where He has acted in ways you never expected. Ask yourself, "If He has been faithful and trustworthy in all those instances, why not count on Him now?"

Give Him control and then watch for the evidence of His faithfulness. He won't let you down.

Today's Choice: Read Psalm 111. What examples of God's trustworthiness and faithfulness does the psalmist give? How is God manifesting His trustworthiness in your life right now?

Reflections:

_____

_____

_____

_____

_____

Moving Mountains

Jesus said, *"Because you have so little faith. Truly I tell you, if you have faith as small as a mustard seed, you can say to this mountain, 'Move from here to there,' and it will move. Nothing will be impossible for you."*

—MATTHEW 17:20

Twice the Lord told His disciples that if they had faith the size of a mustard seed they could do the unbelievable. Apparently, the disciples struggled with that concept. Does that sound familiar? Do you struggle with Jesus' promise too?

In Matthew's gospel, mustard-seed faith is tied to expelling a demon, and Jesus says those who have such faith can move mountains. The disciples wanted that level of faith. You probably do too. But what is the secret of cultivating mountain-moving faith?

Tanya once thought her faith needed to grow to make God pay attention to her request to remove her brother from the homosexual life. But over time she developed a closeness with God. As she learned to come to God on behalf of her brother, her focus shifted from her brother to the God who loved her brother and desired the best for him.

The disciples didn't need great faith, Jesus said. They needed only a little faith—the size of a mustard seed, the smallest seed known in the world. We may think if we had more faith our lives would be different and our loved one would recognize their true sexuality and the identity Christ Jesus designed for them. But Jesus wants us to see that the issue isn't the *amount* of our faith but the *foundation* of our faith. Our faith must be rooted in Him. Bull's-eye!

When we're stuck in our pain and unbelief, we doubt the truth of Matthew 17:20. If we believe nothing will ever change, we'll remain right where we are—mired in that negative, unproductive mindset. That attitude dishonors God because it suggests that God isn't powerful enough to do what He promises or that He isn't trustworthy or that He doesn't care.

When we acknowledge God's greatness, we realize all things are possible, including moving mountains you see as impossible—fractured relationships, broken promises, and destructive addictions. Awesome things happen if we place our full trust in God. Healing and hope can be ours if we remain focused on Him.

Mountain-moving faith is based on God's character and His promises. What promise can you claim today in faith?

Today's Choice: Read Matthew 17:14–21. Examine your heart. What unbelief lurks in it? Ask God to replace your unbelief with confidence in His power.

Reflections:

_____

_____

_____

_____

_____

God Uses Your Pain

So I am willing to endure anything if it will bring salvation and eternal glory in Christ Jesus to those God has chosen.

—2 TIMOTHY 2:10 (NLT)

When we wonder how or why sin came into the world, the Bible leads us back to Adam and Eve. Their disobedience in the garden of Eden permitted the sickness of sin to enter the world. The sin of the those closest to us hurts more because we love them deeply and recognize that the Enemy's deception has taken them into a life that isn't God's best for them. God doesn't want any of us to pursue a rebellious, sinful lifestyle. He loves each of us too much and has shown His love by sacrificing His Son, Jesus Christ.

Lexi considered Casey her best friend. During their childhood, the two shared every success and disappointment with each other—they'd been transparent about everything, or so Lexi thought. But when Casey came out gay to her, Lexi didn't know how to respond. Her heart broke for her friend. All she managed to say was, "You know how much I care and love you." When she got home, she cried and cried. The pain seemed unbearable.

Pain tells us something is wrong and gives us an opportunity to run to God and allow Him to comfort us. Pain also presents the opportunity for the church to come alongside us. Our brothers and sisters in Christ can offer godly support and prayers as they identify with the trials we face. Exposing the depth of our heartache is difficult, but I've learned firsthand the benefits of moving past the fear, thoughts of shame, or judgment of me and my loved one.

Lexi knew she needed to process her pain, but whom could she trust? She called her youth group leaders, Sean and Bethany. Both knew Casey because he'd attended youth group with Lexi the past couple years.

The two leaders met with Lexi. They listened to her heart. After she finished sharing, the three prayed for Casey. They asked God to bring Casey close to Him, to help him know God's love and to cover him with protection as he searched for answers. They also prayed for Lexi and her need for God's comfort, wisdom, strength, and healing as she navigated this journey with her friend.

God was glorified when Lexi allowed others to share her pain and be part of her growth and healing. God was glorified when Sean and Bethany joined Lexi in praying for Casey. That may not be what you want to hear, but as you look down the path ahead, may you see how God is glorified in you and the mighty prayers that spring from your pain for your loved one.

Today's Choice: Read 2 Timothy 2:1–13. Think about the metaphors Paul uses for those who endure hardship for the benefit of others: soldiers, athletes, farmers. With which group do you identify? How is God using your pain to benefit others and bring Him glory?

Reflections:

_____

_____

_____

_____

_____

Know God's Voice

Jesus said, "My sheep hear my voice, and I know them, and they follow me."

—JOHN 10:27

Have you ever asked, "Is that You, God?" when you've heard or sensed a particular message? Some might say your conscience was speaking to you, but maybe the Enemy just wanted you to think that to prevent you from recognizing God's voice.

Jesus told His disciples that His sheep would recognize His voice and follow Him. They would not listen to a stranger's voice or follow him. In fact, Jesus said that "they will run away from him" because they sense the danger of the stranger's presence and the destructiveness of his words (John 10:5).

Sometimes God warns us about something or someone. Once when I walked past a friend, God gave me a warning. I shrugged it off, thinking, where did that come from? But I should have recognized the warning for what it was. Less than a year later, I learned of the deep sexual sin that man was involved in. God attempted to warn me, but I dismissed His counsel. If God warns you of someone or something, He is probably trying to protect you or your family.

Normally, we hear God's voice by reading and studying Scripture. We may also hear His voice in a worship service, when we're taking a quiet walk, or when we converse with a godly mentor or friend.

If you're unsure whether you heard from God, compare the message with what the Holy Spirit has revealed in Scripture. If you feel led to lie to make someone comfortable in their sin or confusion, then you will know you're being deceived, because the Spirit won't contradict what's written in the Word of God.

Second, compare the message with what you know about Jesus. Does the message promote arrogance, lust, or divisiveness? Then it's not the Word of God. You may be shocked at how many bogus "words from God" can be debunked if they are filtered through these two safeguards.

Third, talk to a leader in your church if that helps to give you confidence to follow through on the message. If you're honestly, humbly seeking direction, God will provide the confirmation you need.

God still speaks through the Bible with greater force, greater glory, greater assurance, greater sweetness, greater hope, greater guidance, greater transforming power, and greater Christ-exalting truth than can be heard through any voice in any human soul on the planet. So stay close to your shepherd and learn to recognize His voice.

Today's Choice: Read John 10:1–5. Meditate on the phrase "they know his voice." Ask God to give you an attentive, discerning ear so that you'll learn to run toward Him and away from anyone who attempts to distance you from your shepherd.

Reflections:

_____

_____

_____

_____

_____

Lift Your Eyes to the Hills

I lift up my eyes to the mountains—where does my help come from?
My help comes from the Lord, the Maker of heaven and earth.

—PSALM 121:1–2

I grew up in the heart of Pennsylvania, surrounded by hills and mountains. Their beauty and majesty reminded me of God's great power. He made those mountains. And even when they were hidden by a dense fog, they were still there.

Even though we know Jesus Christ has redeemed us, sometimes when we lift our eyes toward the heavens, we only see thick fog. During those times, God asks us to remember that He is still present and that when the fog clears, we'll see Him clearly again.

As you wait for your fog to clear, lift your eyes to your own hills. What are your own hills? They are your time of greatest darkness and despair, when it seemed God had forgotten you but afterwards you could look back to see that He was really holding you.

For Jesus, the hills He looked to were the cross of Calvary that He had to endure for the joy that He knew was set before Him on the other side. For a dear friend, the hills meant facing the days when she despaired that she would ever recover from the effects of horrific sexual abuse, only to see later that the Lord Jesus was walking with her through her healing journey to the other side. For me, one set of hills I looked to were the ways I'd seen God's power and strength in previous fogs. Each time He directed me into the sunshine again. He proved Himself faithful; He demonstrated that He was the expert guide I needed to lead me.

What are your hills? Are you in them now, crying out for God to be there with you in the darkness? Are you feeling like He has abandoned you? He is closer than you realize.

God knows His hills will provide safety and rest for you. There is nothing wrong with hiding away with God to allow Him to speak to you and minister to you so you don't lose heart. Hold on to hope. Although you struggle with trusting God for allowing this journey into your life, He does ask you to trust Him to finish what He has started. So lift your eyes to the hills and let Him lead you out of the fog.

Today's Choice: Read Psalm 121. This song is one of fifteen psalms (120–134) that God's people sang on their way to Jerusalem to celebrate the annual feasts. In what ways would this psalm provide comfort and courage to travelers? What comfort and courage does it give you on your journey?

Reflections:

_____

_____

_____

_____

_____

Living Life Again

Jesus said to him, "If you can believe, all things are possible to him who believes."

—MARK 9:23 (NKJV)

When a loved one comes out as LGBTQ+, life stops. As family members, we seem to be frozen in time while we watch everyone else continue their normal lives. Neighbors, relatives, and friends go to work, attend church, and take vacations. We, on the other hand, can't take a single step.

Most family members have been in that frozen place, but gradually life returns to some kind of normalcy. Though it seems impossible now, you will move forward again.

The first step is coming to terms with the situation that has affected you so deeply. Accept that your loved one's choices have brought you to your knees and your heart throbs with pain. Staying immobile, however, is not beneficial. Resisting life will only delay your ability to establish new patterns and habits.

As you prepare to live life again, the Enemy will use fear to discourage you from moving forward. Remind yourself that there is no satisfaction in staying where you are any longer. That doesn't mean you push your feelings down or aside. Admit your fear, but don't allow it or your emotions to steal any more from you.

The father in Mark 9 had probably spent countless hours praying that God would heal his son. His words reveal his desperation: "If you can do anything, have compassion on us and help us" (v. 22 NKJV).

Jesus must have detected doubt in that statement because He responded, "If you can believe . . ."

Then the father owned his doubt and told Jesus the truth: "Lord, I believe; help my unbelief!" (v. 24).

Through the power of the Holy Spirit, we can also own our doubt and transform our pattern of thinking from "God isn't hearing my prayers" to "God always hears the prayers of His children." We can switch "my situation will never change" to "God is working even when I don't see evidence of it." We can cry out, "I believe; help my unbelief!"

As you focus on breaking those thought patterns, you'll begin to find joy once again. If you become discouraged, sit down and reflect on the source of your discouragement. Look through your spiritual eyes and ask the Holy Spirit to show you where the Enemy or other people are misdirecting you. This will affirm that the negative emotions are not from God. He never wants us to feel beaten down and hopeless.

You need time to adjust to the new way of thinking, believing, and living. Moving forward to live again may seem intimidating, but you can smile, laugh, and enjoy life again with God's help.

> **Today's Choice:** Read Mark 9:14–29. With whom do you most identify in this story—the powerless disciples, the desperate father, or the tormented son? How did Jesus minister to each of them?

Reflections:

_____

_____

_____

_____

_____

Face the Truth with Courage

Wait on the Lord; Be of good courage, And He shall strengthen your heart;
Wait, I say, on the Lord!

—Psalm 27:14

After Moses died, Joshua was called to lead the people of Israel into the Promised Land. But the new territory held dangers, and the people needed faith and courage to overcome each obstacle. In fact, God told Joshua three times to "be strong and courageous" (Joshua 1: 6, 9). Joshua's faith in God had to be strong to lead the people and to believe God would bring them success in battle against bigger, better-equipped armies.

Sometimes we struggle to believe that we will have success in the battles we face as family members of LGBTQ+ loved ones. Our courage can be shaken by the many complicated situations we must navigate. It takes a lot of courage to take the Word of God for what it says and not waver from it. But the One leading us will not let us down. How do I know?

God did not let Joshua down.

On the night before the Israelites' first battle in the Promised Land, God appeared to Joshua in a vision. Joshua asked, "Are you for us or for our enemies?" (Joshua 5:13)

Dressed as a warrior with sword in hand, God replied, "Neither . . . but as commander of the army of the Lord I have now come" (5:14). God assured Joshua that He, not Joshua, was the commander of Israel's army. Joshua didn't have to go into battle in his own strength or with his own wisdom. God was the commander in chief. That certainty gave Joshua the courage to take on the superior army of Jericho.

God is our commander in chief too. With Him as our leader, we can move forward even if we are afraid. This means we have to be courageous to face reality and what we need or don't need to do. We have to be honest with ourselves, which may be painful. But at the same time, facing truth with courage will bring healing because denial or untruths no longer have a hold on us.

If we show courage like Joshua did, we'll wait patiently for God to do a good work in and for us as well as in and for our loved one. As you discern His plan for the situation, you demonstrate confidence in His ability to direct both your life and your loved one's life. That confidence will increase your courage, generate peace in your mind, and kindle a deeper love for and dependence on God. That is the path to healing.

Today's Choice: Read Joshua 5:13–6:27. What may have seemed impossible about the battle against Jericho? How did Joshua and the Israelite army demonstrate both faith and courage in the battle? What can you do to demonstrate both faith and courage?

Reflections:

_____

_____

_____

_____

_____

Connecting Head and Heart

Say to my soul, "I am your salvation."

—Psalm 35:3

In Psalm 35, David needed to hear from God. He may have known God was his salvation in his head, but he was struggling to fully embrace that truth.

Storing knowledge in our brains is one thing, but storing it in our heart and living by it is different. You may tell God that you're not going to worry but find you can't shake off the worries that plague your mind. There's a disconnect between your head and heart, and you can't bridge it.

Many years after my journey began, I ached for answers to questions about my dad, longing to hear from God. One day, I sat in a California church during some quiet time. I thought of my wedding day. I saw myself standing in the church hallway and preparing to walk up the aisle with my dad. Then he said, "I wish I were in that gown."

Years later, I finally had the courage to ask God, "Where were you when my dad told me he wished he were wearing my wedding gown?" I will never forget the way Jesus calmly brought me back to that moment in complete calmness.

It seemed I was watching a movie, only there was someone new in the scene. Jesus turned my doubt into faith as He gently showed me that He not only was on my left side when my dad spoke but that He also felt profound sadness on my behalf.

As I focused on what Jesus was showing me, I felt peace for the first time about my wedding. The image He showed me then still gives me goose bumps: Jesus walked up the aisle with me while my heart was breaking over my father's words. Jesus also showed me that He, not my dad, gave me away.

Though I felt so alone on my wedding day, I wasn't alone. Though I felt weak, He showed me how strong I was. Though I was broken, Jesus gave me peace and healing.

Sometimes when we reach out to God, He gives us the answers to questions we didn't realize we needed. He says to us as He said to David, "I am your salvation"—"I am the One who walks with you and makes you whole."

God may speak to you in ways you never have imagined. Ask Him to connect what your head is telling you with what your soul needs to hear or be shown. Draw near to Him and don't doubt what He shows you.

Today's Choice: Read Psalm 35. In what ways do you identify with David's situation? David proclaims that "The Lord . . . delights in the well-being of his servant" (v. 27). Do you believe He delights in your well-being? Why?

Reflections:

_____

_____

_____

_____

_____

From Turmoil to Triumph

"I have no peace, no quietness; I have no rest, but only turmoil."

—JOB 3:26

Job's numerous afflictions seem unimaginable to most of us today. In one day, his children were killed, and his livestock destroyed or stolen. Then God allowed Satan to afflict Job with painful boils.

But then a child comes out gay/transgender or a spouse asks for a divorce to pursue an LGBTQ+ lifestyle. In our pain, we identify with Job, who cried out, "Who can see any hope for me?" (Job 17:15).

We may never understand why God permits suffering. But God is for you, not against you. Although that statement may give little comfort now, if you store that truth in your heart, the Holy Spirit will bring it to mind when you're able to process it.

Many Bible characters endured hardship and suffering. David was a fugitive for many years, living in caves as he avoided King Saul's hit men. He grew discouraged and cried out, "Rescue me, Lord, from evildoers . . . who devise evil plans in their hearts and stir up war every day" (Psalm 140:1–2).

Elijah asked for death when he thought Jezebel was going to have him murdered and he felt like he was the only one trying to live righteously (1 Kings 19:4). Moses grew weary of the hard-hearted, complaining Israelites and said to God, "What am I to do with these people? They are almost ready to stone me" (Exodus 17:4).

These examples remind us of Jesus' words in John 16:33, "In this world, you will have trouble." Bible characters had trouble—loads of it. But God also used them to accomplish great things for the kingdom of God. Moses learned to say, "Oh, praise the greatness of our God! He is the Rock, his works are perfect, and all his ways are just" (Deuteronomy 32:3–4). David wrote, "I was young and now I am old, yet I have never seen the righteous forsaken or their children begging bread" (Psalm 37:25). And Job proclaimed,

"I know that my redeemer lives, and . . . I myself will see him with my own eyes" (Job 19:25–27).

They suffered and they recovered. They journeyed through their suffering and then helped others who suffered. They cried out for help, and they shouted out in praise.

God will restore you, too, as you allow Him into your darkest and most heart-wrenching time. The day will come when you'll view your circumstances as an opportunity to grow deeper in love and relationship with the One who wants you to grab hold of faith and embrace new opportunities. And you will praise the greatness of our God.

Today's Choice: Read Psalm 140. In what ways do you identify with the thoughts and feelings David expresses? Which of the verses is most meaningful to you today? Why?

Reflections:

_____

_____

_____

_____

_____

The God Who Answers

But I will sing of your strength; in the morning I will sing of your love:
for you are my fortress, my refuge in times of trouble.

—Psalm 59:16

For thousands of years, God's people have known trouble and distress. Not much has changed about the human condition. God never promised that belonging to Him would mean freedom from trouble. Still, whether your journey has just begun or you've been in crisis mode for some time, you want the crisis to end.

The Bible speaks a lot about faithful servants of God, but none of their lives were trouble-free. So what about those who cried out to God in their crisis? He heard their cries for help, and He hears our prayers too.

God is a wonderful listener. He isn't annoyed or impatient with you; He's eager to help you right where you are. God sees all people, but He sees His children in a special way because He has placed Himself in a covenant of love with them.

The psalms in particular celebrate God's eagerness to hear and help His people in "times of trouble." David testified that God had been to him a "fortress" and a "refuge." (See also Psalm 9:9, 37:39, 41:1).

Our God is at His best in our crises. For example, Anita had just entered her crisis with her son, who had written her a long email, explaining how her faith went against the way he'd chosen to live his life and his decision to marry a man who had transitioned to female. When she read that email, she fell to her knees as if someone had punched her in the gut.

But the truth is, God may want us on our knees. In that position of helplessness, we may allow Him to empty us of self so He can heal the deepest, most hidden areas of our heart. When we feel helpless, we are often more willing to rely on His covenant of love. When we're too weak to argue, we may be more patient as He works out His plan and brings about healing.

God can do far more than we ask or think (Ephesians 3:20). His love for you is great. He always sees you, and He always hears you. He also extends forgiveness when you lapse into unbelief. And He will answer—not necessarily on your timetable or in the way you think your crisis should be handled—but with the answer you need on the day you need it.

So give God your crisis. Your pain will decrease and your confidence in Him will increase as you find refuge in Him and sing of His love.

Today's Choice: Read Psalm 59. Pray verses 9, 16–17 back to the Lord, then wait for Him to fill you with His strength and His love to accomplish today's tasks.

Reflections:

_____

_____

_____

_____

_____

What-Ifs and If-Onlys

My heart says of you, "Seek his face!" Your face, Lord, I will seek.

—PSALM 27:8

At one time or another, you've likely immersed yourself in the sea of what-ifs and if-onlys. What if I had done such and such? Maybe this wouldn't be happening. If only I could change this situation or outcome, then my loved one would do such and such. You aren't alone. We all play that mind game.

Pondering our circumstances may help us process our thoughts and feelings about what's going on in our lives. But the Enemy understands the power of consideration and discernment. He'd much rather we react quickly and instinctively than to think or pray before we respond to our loved one or make assumptions about ourselves. What if I accept Julie or James in their LGBTQ+ world? If only I had been a better parent, spouse, or child then . . .

Many questions we ask ourselves only create more pain. They rarely promote healing because these hypotheticals keep our wounds open. The Enemy of our soul uses them to beat us down and drain our emotional reserves.

If, on the other hand, we invest time in conversation with God, seeking His guidance and listening for His response, the Holy Spirit can help us troubleshoot and find better ways to live and relate. What if I apologized for my initial reaction or the tone of my voice? If only I had waited until I received clear direction from You, Lord, then I may not have acted so rashly.

You don't have to sit in a chair for hours to seek the Lord. Often a physical task will help you unclutter your mind and make it easier to hear God. Lift weights, prepare a meal, clean house, work in the garden. But do these things without the distraction of music or other people. Physical activity frees up space in your brain for alternate kinds of thinking and processing information.

At other times, you'll want to read Scriptures, listening for God to speak about what you struggle with and why. When a particular verse or passage stands out, make note of its location so you can come back to it.

Quiet time with God will help you process all that's going on. Your contemplation and reflection will also give God the opportunity to answer questions and solve problems. You'll discover when physical activity is more helpful than stillness and vice versa. Next time you find yourself wading into the sea of what-ifs and if-onlys, get alone with God. Seek His face. Let Him minster to you.

> **Today's Choice:** Read Psalm 27. What is David's emotional state when the psalm begins? What is his attitude when it ends? In what ways did seeking God's face help him? Set aside some time today to seek God's face and write down what He reveals to you.

Reflections:

_____

_____

_____

_____

_____

Bringing Blessings

And my God will meet all your needs
according to the riches of his glory in Christ Jesus.

—PHILIPPIANS 4:19

Christians often say "what a blessing" because we believe the gift received—tangible or intangible—is from God. But when a loved one's decisions consume our mind and heart with worry and concern, we may find it difficult to see God's blessings.

In our most painful times, however, we often experience God's richest blessings: a stronger faith, a deeper love for God, and a more intimate walk with Him. Our trials ground our faith in ways that prosperity and abundance never could.

Laura Story's song "Blessings" invites us to consider that God's mercies can be disguised as fierce storms and dark nights. You may not be able to view your situation that way yet, but as you allow God to step beside, in front of, and behind you, you will come to see your journey as what the song describes as "mercies in disguise."

Sometimes we have to step back to gain some perspective. I'm learning that my perspective must be long-long-term. In many instances, a trial passes and you move on—a better, stronger, and more joyous person for having passed through that difficulty. That's living in a long-term perspective.

But in other cases, the trial continues for a lifetime. History records the stories of many martyrs who endured decades of suffering only to have that suffering end in death. That kind of trial requires a long-long-term perspective—a perspective that recognizes relief might not come until the next life. If that thought makes you want to cry (or scream), hang on. Good news is coming.

The apostle Paul wrote the book of Philippians in prison, and yet he was able to say, "I have learned to be content whatever the circumstances" (4:11).

How could he say that and mean it? He had developed the long-long-term perspective: "I can do all this through him who gives me strength" (4:13). The blessing of strength God provided each day enabled Paul to find joy in the support he received from the Philippians and in their spiritual growth (4:14–20).

God hasn't promised any of us that we'll avoid suffering—or even a martyr's death. Each of us, therefore, needs to gain a long-long-term perspective. Perhaps you'll be one of the few who sails through life with few trials. But don't count on it; the odds are against you. On the other hand, if you gain that long-long-term perspective, then you'll learn to find joy in life's smallest gifts. And, even more important, you'll learn to bring joy to others, despite your pain.

Today's Choice: Read Philippians 4:10–20. What blessings did Paul celebrate in prison? What blessings can you celebrate today?

Reflections:

_____

_____

_____

_____

_____

What's the Next Step?

Jesus said, *"Come to Me, all you who labor and are heavy laden, and I will give you rest. Take My yoke upon you and learn from Me, for I am gentle and lowly in heart, and you will find rest for your souls. For My yoke is easy and My burden is light."*

—Matthew 11:28–30 (NKJV)

As we look for answers to solve problems or change circumstances, we may ask, "What's the next step?"

Jesus gave His listeners a simple answer: "Come to Me." Sounds too simplistic, doesn't it? The truth is, we sometimes make a decision more difficult because we try to control the situation or another person. But we are not our savior—or anyone else's. That's why Jesus said, "Come to Me."

Will we believe Jesus and His promise to give us rest and bear our burden, or will we ignore Him and step forward on our own?

In a culture of instant gratification and quick fixes, we've become addicted to immediate results. We pull into the drive-thru lane, order a meal, pay for it, and start eating it in minutes. If the checkout line at the grocery store has more than one person in it, we move over to the self-checkout lane. We assume that whatever is quick and easy is the best choice.

But that's not Jesus' mindset. He has infinite patience and is more than willing to wait calmly, arms open wide, for us to stop and turn to him. He is seldom interested in quick fixes; He'd much rather allow our souls to marinate in our circumstances until we're willing to take His yoke.

When we attempt to gain what we want in our own strength—as quickly as possible—we demonstrate our lack of faith in Jesus and our struggle intensifies. We feel "heavy laden" because we're trying to lift the unliftable. Our spirit, mind, will, and emotions can't function properly either, which may lead to depression, anxiety, loneliness, and hopelessness.

Under the weight of our circumstances, we wrongly assume that Jesus isn't interested in helping us. But He doesn't want us to focus on the how and when—as if we are wise enough to understand and determine them. He prefers that we rest in Him, confident that He knows what's best for us and our loved ones. If we allow Him to lift our burden and slip His yoke of obedience over our shoulders, we will feel lighter. His gentleness and love will soothe us, and His peace will give us hope.

When the question "what next?" arises in your mind, answer it with "go to Jesus." Rest in His presence until He lifts the burden and shows you the next step.

Today's Choice: Read Matthew 11:25–30. Do Jesus' words in verses 25–27 make it easier or harder for you to give your burdens to Him? Why?

Reflections:

_____

_____

_____

_____

_____

Love My Enemies?

"You have heard that it was said, 'You shall love your neighbor and hate your enemy.' But I say to you, love your enemies and pray for those who persecute you."

—MATTHEW 5:43

Walking our journey with loved ones identifying under the LGBTQ+ label, we may run into roadblocks. These obstacles may become more hazardous when we're upset with the LGBTQ+ alliance or some other advocacy organization. We see those groups as part of the problem, or we blame its members for our loved one's waywardness and pain.

One day when I walked into my dad's hospital room, a group of friends surrounded his bed. They attended the church that supported the life he was living and embraced him as female. Anger welled up in me as I listened to them call him Becky, her, or she. How could they support my dad's deception and propel him further into his delusion? I resented the church leadership's decision to support this ideology instead of guiding my dad to a deeper relationship with God, a Father who loved him so deeply and desired healing for him.

If we obey God's commandment to love our enemies, we will work diligently to release our anger and hurt over the influence others have played in our loved one's life. Loving our enemies does not mean we have to like everything about them; however, we can develop a better understanding of God's love for us and for them as we learn to love those we blame or strongly dislike because of our situation and our loved one's decisions.

Jesus' command is difficult to live out but worth pursuing, especially in a culture infested with enmity. Who knows? To love our enemies may be the way to propel us over the roadblock so we can go where God wants to take us.

In my case, I developed a relationship with the friends who stood in my dad's hospital room. I either had a discussion with them surrounding the need to minster to the hurting heart and soul in those like my dad, or God gave me the opportunity to respect them when we talked about cleaning out my dad's home and taking care of his final arrangements.

God doesn't allow roadblocks to keep us from Him but to draw us closer to Him. How can you move past the obstacle of viewing people or organizations as your enemies? Spend time in prayer, seeking God earnestly for His help to love those you don't want to love. If you view others as enemies, treat them with respect and offer them the same compassion Jesus Christ offers you. When possible, make every effort to know and understand them better. Protect your heart from judging them. Remember, they may be blinded by Satan, just as you and I once were.

Today's Choice: Read Matthew 5:43–48. According to verse 44, what is one way to cultivate love for those we consider enemies? (Note: the word translated *perfect* in verse 48 implies growth, suggesting that loving our enemies is a lifelong process.)

Reflections:

_____

_____

_____

_____

_____

Turning the Page

Now the Lord said to Samuel, "How long will you mourn for Saul? . . . I am sending you to Jesse the Bethlehemite. For I have provided Myself a king among his sons."

—1 Samuel 16:1 (NKJV)

S ometimes the greatest roadblock to deepening your relationship with God today is your refusal to let go of yesterday's mistakes and doubts. You can't step forward if you remain in the past. Letting go of the past enables us to move into the future God has planned.

Samuel had anointed Saul king of Israel. He loved Saul, counseled him, and interceded for him. But Saul chose to reject God's plan for his life. So God chose another king—David, the youngest son of Jesse the Bethlehemite. In 1 Samuel 16, God commands Samuel to turn the page on the past. Time to move on.

What about your past is blocking your future?

One of the false recommendations a family member, friend, or colleague can make is that you should be on the other side of your pain—as if God designates a specific amount of time for us to process and work through our disappointments and losses. Take the time you need to grieve, but don't get stuck there.

God allowed Samuel to grieve, but then He made it clear that Samuel needed to move on to the next assignment. God knew that anointing David as the next king would give Samuel the hope he needed to continue to serve God and the nation of Israel. God knows what will fuel your hope and sense of purpose too.

Samuel obeyed God. He did the hard thing and went to Bethlehem to anoint David. God protected Samuel on the journey, then clearly revealed which of Jesse's sons was the chosen one. God also affirmed the choice in a way Samuel couldn't miss: "So Samuel took the horn of oil and anointed

[David] . . . and from that day on the Spirit of the Lord came powerfully upon David"(1 Samuel 16:13).

Take ownership of where God is leading you. Follow His direction. God wants victory for you. If you allow Him access to your heart, He will help you live out the plan He has ordained for you with joy, hope, and purpose.

As you begin to move forward, you'll recognize more easily how God operates to protect you and to reveal how He has worked around past disappointments and failure. Turn the page on the past. Look ahead to what God will do in your life today and tomorrow. Claim the promise of His presence and wait for a demonstration of His power that will confirm His delight in your obedience.

Today's Choice: Read 1 Samuel 16:1–13. What did Samuel have to let go of in order to move forward? What might God be asking you to let go of?

Reflections:

_____

_____

_____

_____

_____

Press On

Not that I have already obtained it or have already become perfect, but I press on so that I may lay hold of that for which also I was laid hold of by Christ Jesus.

—Philippians 3:12 (NASB)

I don't know what your story is, where you've been, what you've done, or what has been done to you. But God's Word teaches that God did not place you in this circumstance and this time without a plan and a purpose. Ultimately, everything God permits has purpose.

If you take one step forward—no matter how small or difficult—you'll see how God uses that step to glorify Himself and advance His kingdom. Any single step may have eternal impact. God's ways are not our ways. He's not looking for obvious external qualifications or results. God looks at the heart, your heart.

To grow as a Christian, we must stay in the race, running toward God not away from Him. Before the apostle Paul met Jesus on the road to Damascus, he thought he was doing everything he needed to do to please God. He was wrong. God reached down to redirect Paul and transformed his life.

Years later, Paul clarified that behind his effort to "press on" is the foundational fact of being "laid hold of by Jesus Christ." The phrase "laid hold of" means to apprehend or seize something you're going after. Paul ran the race because Christ Jesus chased him down. After the Damascus Road encounter, Paul began to serve Jesus—passionately, steadfastly.

If you've not been "laid hold of by Christ Jesus," you're not in the race. The Christian life begins with the commitment to follow God. Christian growth comes from definite awareness of being apprehended by Christ Jesus.

When Zack learned his brother was identifying and living as a woman, Zack struggled with his attitude toward God for permitting this situation. But Zack had committed his life to Jesus, so he allowed Him to look into his heart and reveal the poor attitude he carried with him every day. Attitude is a crucial aspect in spiritual growth, and to run the race, Zack had to adjust his mindset. The Greek word translated "to think" or "be minded" is used ten times in Philippians, highlighting the importance of attitude.

Spiritual growth is a lifelong process. None of us will ever be able to say, "I've arrived." The right attitude facilitates forward progress. Don't give distress, grief, and worry the power to stop you. Expect to be stretched but press on. As you allow God to take hold of you, you will be able to run your race.

Today's Choice: Read Philippians 3:10–16. What does Paul say motivated him to press on? What motivates you?

Reflections:

_____

_____

_____

_____

_____

Support for You

Let each of us please his neighbor for his good, to build him up.

—Romans 15:2 (ESV)

The Bible is a book of relationships. Its guidelines reveal what our relationship to God is meant to be and how to develop that kind of relationship with Him; Scripture also shows us how to interact with our fellow Christians and anyone who is hurting—including ourselves. Godly love and relationships are essential on our journey alongside an LGBTQ+ loved one.

Every human being wants to be loved, to be special to someone. God created us to be relational. But sometimes when our needs seem so great, we tell ourselves we can walk our journey alone. At one time, I told myself that lie. I chose the difficult path of solitude out of grief and shame as well as an unwillingness to trust others. I wished that I could go to someone for comfort and understanding, but I resisted.

Christian families are bombarded by ungodly cultural influences, and even some churches have embraced the lie that love means approval. But God's Word does not change, and we need a group of likeminded, godly companions who'll stand firm on His Word. Support systems or groups can be part of our healing if we're willing to trust them and reject the Enemy's attempts to hinder our spiritual and emotional healing.

Maybe these testimonies will encourage you to reach out:

- Kassie struggled alone for seven years with her daughter's lesbian relationships before she reached out to me. She said, "I can't believe how light I feel compared to the heaviness before we spoke."
- Derek: "I felt like I was the only dad going through my situation until I joined the support group."
- Chrissy: "When my sister came out as gay, I thought I had nowhere to turn. I'm so glad I've found a support group."

- Douglas: "When we found out our son was transitioning, I believed no one understood. I was wrong."
- Debra: "Being with other moms living through the same thing has ministered to me deeply."
- Tasha: "I never spoke to another child who went through what I had with my dad's life-altering decision. Your support has been invaluable."

If you don't have a support system, ask yourself why. If you're ashamed, what is causing it? If you're mistrustful, is it justified or irrational? If you're grieving, why not allow others to grieve with you?

God doesn't want you to stay where you are. Your pain can help you have deeper compassion for anyone who's hurting. He wants you to allow others to build you up, and He wants to use you to build them up.

Today's Choice: Read Romans 15:1–7. Do you consider yourself strong or weak? If you feel strong, what does Paul encourage you to do? If you feel weak, what is he counseling you to do?

Reflections:

_____

_____

_____

_____

_____

Equipped to Endure

We are hard-pressed on every side, yet not crushed; we are perplexed,
but not in despair; persecuted, but not forsaken; struck down, but not destroyed.

—2 Corinthians 4:8–9 (NKJV)

D o you battle disappointment—not only with yourself or others but also with God?

When we don't understand God's perspective or His reasons for allowing our troubles, we may feel that He has let us down. If we conclude that He isn't willing or able to help us, we may consider giving up.

But that's not what Paul tells us to do in the tough times. Paul had lived through a lot of danger and pain—beaten with rods, accused of crimes, slandered by opponents. But he didn't quit. He knew God had redeemed him, called him into ministry, and equipped him with the Holy Spirit. He began each of his letters with this kind of affirmation: "Paul, an apostle of Christ Jesus by the will of God" (2 Corinthians 1:1). Past difficulty didn't stop Paul from stepping forward in faith the next day.

God has provided us with the same salvation, calling, and equipping. But we need to live as redeemed, called, and equipped children of God. We need to claim the power and purpose God makes available to us. We cannot allow the Enemy to convince us that God is asking us to do something impossible.

If we focus on what God has given us, we're less likely to give up. We may not understand everything about our situation or our calling, but a commitment to endure doesn't require understanding. We persevere because we believe God is loving, wise, and present—just as Paul did.

The journey of a loved one living under the LGBTQ+ umbrella is difficult. Tears have streamed down your face and your heart has ached. Maybe you've stayed in bed all day or refused to answer the front door when a friend came calling. But past actions don't dictate future ones. Determine to do one thing God has called you to do today—whether it's doing laundry, attending a Bible study, or cooking a meal at a soup kitchen. As you do that task, He'll provide the strength for the next one. And the next. That's how you move from "hard-pressed on every side" to "yet not crushed."

Because Paul didn't give up, people heard the gospel and accepted Jesus as savior. Churches were established across the Middle East and Europe. Set aside what you're facing and how discouraging it is. Take hold of the gifts God has given you and affirm His presence in your circumstances. The blessings of your perseverance and faithfulness may be right around the corner.

Today's Choice: Meditate on 2 Corinthians 4:8–9. What is crushing you today? What is perplexing you today? Write them down, then burn the paper as a symbol that you are giving those things to God and that they will not keep you from stepping forward in faith today.

Reflections:

_____

_____

_____

_____

_____

Seeing God's Goodness

The sun rose above him as he passed Peniel,
and he was limping because of his hip.

—Genesis 32:31

Have you ever been so weary that you said, "I cannot take another step"? Have you awakened in the morning and refused to open your eyes because you still felt exhausted?

Pain can do that. It can weaken us to the point that we're immobile. It can fill our heart with so much darkness that we cannot feel the sun. It can twist our faith in God into a tangle of doubt. You're not the only one who has felt that way. I've been there. So have many others. The Bible also records the stories of many who reached that point.

Scripture says that one night Jacob was "left alone, and a man wrestled with him till daybreak" (Genesis 32:24). Was this man an angel or God Himself? The Bible doesn't say. But after many hours, the man "touched the socket of Jacob's hip so that his hip was wrenched" (v. 25).

Jacob was debilitated in a matter of seconds during this life-changing battle. And although the pain was probably excruciating, Jacob held on to the man and said, "I will not let you go unless you bless me" (v. 26).

In response, the man gave him a new name: Israel. Jacob had always been known as a deceiver, but after his experience with the man from heaven, he was known as the one who struggled with God. And Jacob's new name became the name of the nation of God's people.

The name change was a demonstration of God's promise-keeping goodness at work. The promise God had given to Abraham in Genesis 12:1—"I will make you into a great nation"—would be fulfilled. Jacob's twelves sons and their descendants became that nation.

God's goodness can also be seen in Jacob's dislocated hip. The injury may not ever have healed completely, and Jacob probably walked with a limp for the rest of his days. The limp became a lifelong reminder of his weakness and God's superior strength.

The struggle and the injury brought good—not only to Jacob but also to his descendants down through the centuries and to us who follow Christ now.

Your current struggle and the injuries that may result can also bring about good. If you cannot see any goodness, then ask God to adjust your perspective. Don't be surprised if a wrestling match follows, but also be confident that blessings will follow too.

Today's Choice: Read Genesis 32:22–31. Have you ever had a mental wrestling match with God? What was the reason for the struggle? What was the result?

Reflections:

_____

_____

_____

_____

_____

Share Your Story

*Now I want you to know, brothers and sisters, that what has happened to me
has actually served to advance the gospel.*

—Philippians 1:12

You may think your story isn't significant enough to share with others or that your experience is too isolated to influence others, but that isn't what the Bible teaches through the stories of people such as Esther.

Through her Uncle Mordecai, God says that Esther was born "for such a time"—divinely placed in her situation to save the Jews from destruction (Esther 4:14). What did she do? She courageously spoke the truth when it would have been much easier and much safer to remain silent.

God desires that we follow Esther's example.

What has God shown you through your journey? What truths about His faithfulness, provision, and protection could you share with others? More than likely, you're not the same person you used to be. Your faith has grown, and your relationship with God has deepened. Speaking about your journey in private or public settings may seem scary, but God can use your words to enlighten and encourage others. Every trial, setback, and success are opportunities to share a testimony of how God worked in your life and made you stronger.

God has hand-tailored your story specifically for you to shape you into the person He wants you to become. But what you do with your story— whether you share it with one person or a million people—may inspire someone who is struggling with their faith in God and His healing touch.

If you've heard incredible testimonies in church services, on TV shows, or in books, you may conclude that those remarkable stories of transformation are the only ones worth telling. But that isn't true. Every story of God's faithfulness is worth sharing because each one glorifies His name and proclaims the truth.

Your story may help others better understand LGBTQ+ issues or how a family is impacted when a loved ones pursues that lifestyle. Your faith in God may motivate someone else to persevere in a very different trial than your own. As you share how others have comforted and supported you, you may encourage someone to extend compassion and assistance to others who are hurting. Your story may help others know they are not alone and may unlock the door of their prison of shame, grief, or regret.

You've made it this far because of God. Share His faithfulness with others, and perhaps He'll use your words to advance the gospel and prompt someone else to accept Jesus Christ as Savior.

Today's Choice: Read Philippians 1:12–18. According to verse 18, what was "the important thing" for Paul? What is the important thing for you?

Reflections:

_____

_____

_____

_____

_____

Forever Changed

Then a man of God came and spoke to the king of Israel, and said, Thus says the Lord: Because the Syrians have said, "The Lord is God of the hills, but He is not God of the valleys, therefore I will deliver all this great multitude into your hand, and you shall know that I am the Lord."

—1 KING 20:28 (NKJV)

We walk into a brighter morning and a better day when we acknowledge the inner changes God is bringing about regarding who we are and what we believe because of what we have experienced. We are also more aware of God's presence as we look back and see where we were when we first learned of our loved one's LGBTQ+ identification and decisions.

We can develop an even greater awareness of God's presence by reaching out to Him in all situations—both hills and valleys. In 1 Kings 20:28, the Syrians assumed that the Lord was "a god of the hills and not a god of the valleys," so He showed them His power in the valley and delivered them into the hands of the Israelite army so all of them would learn "that I am the Lord."

Hills and valleys are a part of everyone's faith journey. As we recognize God's sovereignty over the high and low places in our lives, we learn to access His peace and joy in every circumstance.

You may think hills only represent times of celebration—weddings, births, family reunions, graduations, and job promotions. But hills can also be quiet walks with a loved one, meals with friends, or brilliant sunsets. Most of us recognize hills as God's blessings. These hilltop experiences help us recall His goodness and faithfulness when He leads us through the valleys.

Dark, treacherous times can make us believe God has left us, but in reality, He is closest to us in these valleys. Because we slow down—maybe even stop—during these times, God is better able to begin the transformation of our heart and soul. The change comes slowly, but rest assured it does come as we sit in silence and reflect on our powerful God, who rules with absolute sovereignty. And because we have experienced His power on the hilltops, we can be confident that His power is equally effective in the valleys.

As God changes you, He will continue to help you through your uncertainties and pain. He never changes. He keeps pace with us as we ascend the hills and stumble through the valleys, and He will finish the good work He has begun in each of us (Philippians 1:6).

The transformation He is bringing about in you is a forever change. I know because of what He's done for me and for many others whom I've met on my journey. Give God time. Keep in step with Him. Allow Him to transform you forever.

> **Today's Choice:** Read 1 Kings 20:22–30. How did the Syrians' misconceptions about the God of Israel lead to their destruction? What misconceptions about God did you have earlier in your faith journey? How did He help you see the truth?

Reflections:

_____

_____

_____

_____

_____

It's All about Faith

The fundamental fact of existence is that this trust in God, this faith,
is the firm foundation under everything that makes life worth living.

—Hebrews 11:1 (MSG)

Early one morning Grace awoke suddenly, her heart racing and her palms sweaty. Fear welled up inside her. She took a few deep breaths and said, "I know You are with me, God. Help." Her breathing steadied and her heartbeat slowed. The fear disappeared.

God was with Grace that morning. He is with her every morning. He is with you too.

In the Bible, God assures us that He will never leave or forsake us (Deuteronomy 31:6; Hebrews 13:5). He promises to walk with us through the "valley of the shadow of death" and through the "deep waters" and the "fire" (Psalm 23:4; Isaiah 43:2 NKJV). God is our "ever-present help in trouble," wrote the psalmist (Psalm 46:1). He is the "God of all comfort," and the God who says, "I have loved you with an everlasting love" (2 Corinthians 1:3; Jeremiah 31:3).

We can count on Him. Always.

There is no *if* when it comes to hard times—only *when* and *what kind.* They will arrive at our doorstep uninvited and may be unwelcome guests for a long, long while. God knows life will be hard. That's why He gave us the Bible—full of His promises to steady us and packed with wisdom to guide us.

The Enemy, however, will use every trick possible to create chaos and destruction. When we acknowledge what's happening and who's behind it, we need to follow Grace's example and say, "I know You are with me, God" and ask for help.

No power in the universe can stop God from hearing our plea or coming to our aid. But we also must place full confidence in His timing. We don't know everything He knows; we can't see everything He sees. Perhaps, like in a game of chess, God is moving things and people around to bring you the answer to your prayers.

Our journey comes down to faith. Faith means accepting that God knows best despite what we think we see or what we believe is the best way to take care of ourselves or our loved ones. Faith is all about seeing the impossible as possible. Will we hold on to our trust in God and prove ourselves faithful servants, or will we leave the safety of His presence and attempt to fight the Enemy and heal our wounds by ourselves?

As you continue your journey, may each day bring you a greater awareness of God's presence, His care, and His love. He is with you. You can count on it.

Today's Choice: Read Hebrews 11:1–40. Which of the men and women mentioned in this chapter do you most relate to? Why? What does that person's example motivate you to do today?

Reflections:

_____

_____

_____

_____

_____

We're Here for You

I often think of the Enemy's satisfaction when family members stay closed off from others and hide behind the walls of their home while they hurt so badly. I know what that's like. I hid because of shame, embarrassment, and lack of trust for many years. I was not moving forward to experience healing. Then one day I became mad. I was mad at myself for giving Satan exactly what he wanted: keep me away from support and healing on my journey. If you need others to stand with you through prayer and support, please consider calling or emailing us. We want to serve you and to be a part of your journey.

Help 4 Families Ministry
phone: 814-598-4952
email: care@help4families.com

Living Stones Ministries
phone 626-963-6683
email: info@livingstonesministry.org

Other Books by

Your True Identity: How Freedom in Christ Brings Healing, Hope, and Wholeness provides a biblical perspective on gender and sexuality for those who struggle with gender identity, transsexual confusion, and same-sex or opposite-sex compulsions.

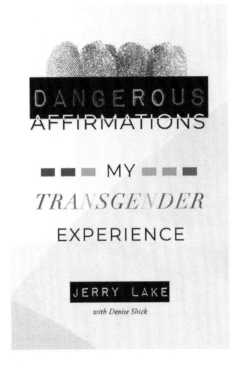

Dangerous Affirmations is a personal story of a young boy who shares his struggle of living in his male gender. As a child, his grandmother dressed him in a dress, while his father affirmed him looking pretty. *Dangerous Affirmations* addresses this from a Christian standpoint.

There is a great deal of mystery and confusion about how to deal with transgenderism in the Christian community. *When Hope Seems Lost* provides churches and families with a biblical response to transgenderism.

Transgender Confusion – A Biblical Q&A for Families

Having a loved one who identifies as the opposite gender is challenging. Family members face situations that will stretch each one's emotional and spiritual strength. I remember the first time I opened a Bible in search for answers. The Bible does not use the word transgenderism, but it does talk about our minds becoming a battlefield. So where do we go to bring clarity? We go to God's word. He addresses the fleshly desires and reminds us "our struggle is not against flesh and blood, but against the rulers, against the authorities, against the powers of this dark world and against the spiritual forces of evil in the heavenly realms" (Ephesians 6:12–13).

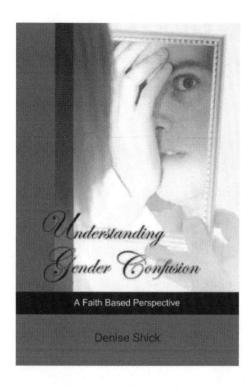

Understanding Gender Confusion

Sometimes people think if they pray or wish hard enough, their transgender tendencies will disappear. This is an unrealistic expectation. It is not reasonable to expect an overnight change in the area of gender or sexual confusion. The problem takes years to develop. Likewise, the restoration process requires a lengthy healing and hard work,-which typically involves years of serious commitment.

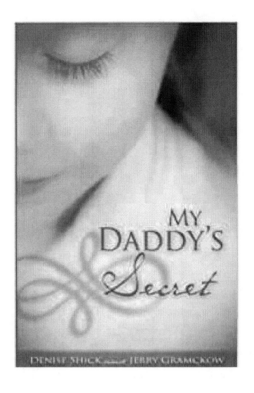

My Daddy's Secret is the sensitive, often heartbreaking, true story of the effects of a father's secret sexual addictions on his family—particularly on his oldest daughter, whom he made his confidante when she was just nine years old. The author hopes this book will provide new insights into the pain such addictions inflict on families and insight into God's amazing grace in healing those pains.

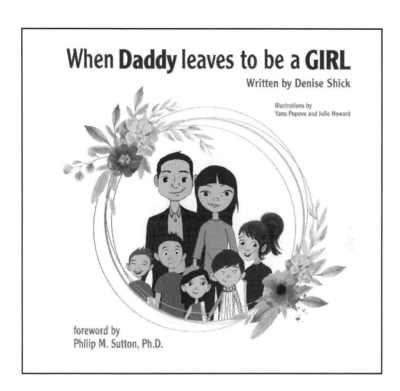

When **Daddy** leaves to be a **GIRL**

Written by Denise Shick

Illustrations by
Yana Popova and Julie Howard

foreword by
Philip M. Sutton, Ph.D.

When Daddy Leaves to Be a Girl can help children handle the emotional turmoil of learning that their parent wants to transition to another sex. In age-appropriate language, Denise Shick explores the fears, confusion, and anger a child may experience during these difficult circumstances. She offers children assurance that God sees their pain and loves them. She also gives practical ways to guide children toward emotional and spiritual wholeness.

What's Up with Cousin Stacy? explores one family's response to the news of a loved one identifying as LGBT. With his parents' help, Kevin learns that love, honesty, and prayer are the best ways to navigate stressful situations.

This book is a valuable tool for parents, pastors, and counselors who seek to demonstrate love and compassion as they help families process and respond to a loved one's decision to identify as LGBT.

In *I'm Glad Made Me a Girl*, young girls discover God's design and purpose for them. The story also touches on the reasons some girls believe becoming a boy makes sense for them. This resource shows girls that they are fearfully and wonderfully made by God and that as females, they are beautiful, kind, brave, smart, and strong.

The Boy Who Liked Tea Parties gently explores ways families can guide a child toward healthy gender identity and development. It is a valuable tool for parents, pastors, and counselors who seek to demonstrate love and compassion as they help children develop gender confidence.

Made in the USA
Columbia, SC
07 January 2024